ABSTRACT

The global demand for energy is growing day by day. The best source of energy that can be chosen is renewable energy. Solar energy is available in abundance. It is clean and inexhaustible. Due to these advantages, solar energy can be used to satisfy the increasing demand. This is done using Photovoltaic (PV) systems. PV systems have nonlinear characteristics due to insolation and temperature dependence. They are expensive and also energy conversion efficiency is very low. Maximum Power Point Tracking (MPPT) is used to increase the efficiency of the system. This ensures that maximum available power is extracted under varying environmental conditions. Various techniques like Perturb and Observe (P&O) and Incremental Conductance (InC) exist. But problems of oscillations and convergence occur at certain points during tracking. Also these techniques do not perform well under partial shading conditions.

Therefore, a technique named 'Particle Swarm

Optimization'

(PSO) has been chosen to improve the efficiency of

tracking process. Also, PSO performs well under partial shading conditions. This project presents a

comparison between conventional P&O technique and PSO using a SIMULINK/MATLAB model. The simulation model shows that PSO technique is better than that of conventional P&O. Hardware implementation has been done and the results are discussed.

(iii)

LIST OF TABLES

TABLE NO. TABLE TITLE   PAGE NO.

LIST OF ABBREVIATIONS AND SYMBOLS

GHG-Green House Gas

PV- Photo Voltaic

V_{oc} - Open Circuit Voltage

I_{sc}- Short Circuit Current

MPPT- Maximum Power Point Tracking

I_{MPP}, V_{MPP}- Current and Voltage at which maximum power occurs

P&O- Perturb and Observe

InC- Incremental Conductance

FOCV- Fractional Open Circuit Voltage

ANN- Artificial Neural Network

ACO- Ant Colony Optimisation

GA- Genetic Algorithm

PSO - Particle Swarm Optimization

MA

TL

AB

-

MA

Tri

x

LA

Bor

ator

y

GN

D-

Gro

und

.

ADC-Analog to Digital Converter

LDR -Light Dependent Resistor

LCD-Liquid Crystal Display

CV- Constant Voltage

SC-Short Circuit

CHAPTER 1

INTRODUCTION

Conventional energy sources based on oil, coal, and natural gas have proven to be highly effective drivers of economic progress, but at the same time damaging to the environment and to human health. These traditional fossil fuel-based energy sources are facing increasing pressure on a host of environmental fronts, with perhaps the most serious challenge confronting the future use of coal being the Kyoto Protocol greenhouse gas (GHG) reduction targets. Any effort to maintain atmospheric levels of CO_2 below even 550 ppm cannot be based fundamentally on an oil and coal-powered global economy, barring radical carbon sequestration efforts. Thus, Renewable Energy is the alternative to conventional sources.

1.1 Renewable Energy

Renewable Energy comes from natural sources that are constantly and sustainably replenished. It is the best alternative to cover the world's increasing demand for electricity in view of the increasing fossil fuel prices and expected negative climate impact due to increased burning fossil fuels. It is more economic to harvest the good resources and convert them to electricity to be transported to the regions where electricity is needed, rather than using poor resources found near the demand. Renewables contributed 19 percent to our energy consumption and 22 percent to our electricity generation in 2012 and 2013, respectively.

The potential of renewable energy sources is enormous as they can in principle meet many times the world's energy demand. Renewable Energy sources such as biomass, wind, solar, hydropower, and geothermal can provide sustainable energy services, based on the use of routinely available, indigenous resources. A transition to renewables-based energy systems is looking increasingly likely as the costs of solar and wind power systems have dropped substantially in the past 30 years, and continue to decline, while the price of oil and gas continue to fluctuate.

1.1.1 Goal of using Renewable energy

The goal in using renewable energy sources is to reduce the negative environmental effects associated with non-renewable energy sources such as coal and natural gas.Opting to use a renewable energy source will not only translate into cost savings over the long haul, but will also help protect the environment from the risks of fossil fuel emissions of non-renewable energy sources.

1.1.2 Advantages of Renewable energy

The advantages of Renewable energy are

- One major advantage with the use of renewable energy is that as it is renewable it is therefore sustainable and so will never run out.
- It produces little or no waste products such as carbon dioxide or other chemical pollutants, so it has minimal impact on the environment.
- Renewable energy facilities generally require less maintenance than traditional generators. Their fuel being derived from natural and available resources reduces the costs of operation.

1.1.3 Types of Renewable energy

The types of Renewable energy are

- Solar energy
- Wind energy
- Biogas energy
- Geothermal energy
- Hydropower
- Biomass energy and cellulosic ethanol
- Wave and tidal energy

1.2 Solar Energy

Every day, the sun radiates an enormous amount of energy called Solar energy. Only a small part of the visible radiant energy (light) that the sun emits into space ever reaches the Earth, but that is more than enough to supply all our energy needs. Every hour enough Solar energy reaches the Earth to supply our energy needs. Solar energy is considered a renewable energy source due to this fact. Solar energy is a clean and renewable energy source, which produces neither greenhouse effect gases nor hazardous wastes through its utilization. It is clean, inexhaustible, and abundant in nature. Wide installation of renewable energy systems helps to keep our environment clean and healthy. World energy demand has been increasing in the past few years due to the world economic growth and population increase, especially in developing countries.

Conventional methods of generating electricity can produce pollutants such as Carbon dioxide, the main gas responsible for global warming. Thus, Solar energy is used to produce electricity. Two ways to make electricity from Solar energy are Photovoltaics and Solar thermal systems. The sun is a constant natural source of heat and light, and its radiation can be converted to electricity. According to estimates, 35 MW of power could be generated from 1 sq km.

1.2.1 Advantages of Solar energy

The advantages of Solar energy are

1. Solar energy is free although there is a cost in the building of 'collectors' and other equipment required to convert solar energy into electricity or hot water.
2. Solar energy does not cause pollution.
3. Solar energy can be used in remote areas where it is too expensive to extend the electricity power grid.
4. Many everyday items such as calculators and other low power consuming devices can be powered by solar energy effectively.
5. It is estimated that the world's oil reserves will last for 30 to 40 years. On the other hand, solar energy is infinite.

Solar energy is more readily available than wind or other forms of renewable energy. Therefore, use of Solar energy will increase countries' energy security through reliance on an indigenous, inexhaustible and mostly import independent resource, enhance sustainability, reduce pollution, lower the costs of mitigating global warming, and keep fossil fuel prices lower than otherwise.

CHAPTER 2
PHOTOVOLTAIC CELL

The sun's light energy can be converted directly into electricity in a single process using Photovoltaic (PV) cells. These cells are made of semiconductor materials, such as silicon, whichexhibit a property known as the photoelectric effect that causes them to absorb photons of light and release electrons.

2.1 Photoelectric effect

It is the ability of some semiconductors to convert electromagnetic radiation directly into electrical current. The charged particles generated by the incident radiation are separated conveniently to create an electrical current. This effect can be attributed to the transfer of energy from the light to an electron in the metal.

2.2 Photovoltaic (PV) cell

Photovoltaic (PV) cells convert sun's light energy directly into electricity. A PV cell is a thin plate of light sensitive material made primarily of silicon. They have a working life of 20 -30 years. Individual PV cells vary in size from about 1 cm to about 10 cm across. A cell of this size can only produce 1 or 2 watts, which is not enough power for most applications. To increase power output, cells are electrically connected into a module. Modules are connected to form an array. The term "array" refers to the entire generating plant, whether it is made up of one or several thousand modules.The performance of a photovoltaic array is dependent upon sunlight. Climate (e.g. clouds, fog) has a significant effect on the amount of solar energy received by a PV array and, in turn, its performance. Local defects, such as a locally reduced diffusion length, a strong local shunt resistance or a high local series resistance will adversely influence the cell's global properties. Most commercial photovoltaic modules are about 10 - 15% percent efficient in converting sunlight to electricity with further research being conducted to raise this efficiency. Experimental cells with conversion efficiencies in excess of 30 per cent are now possible.

2.3 Advantages of photovoltaic conversion for power generation

The advantages of photovoltaic conversion for power generation are

- Conversion from sunlight to electricity is direct, so that bulky mechanical generator systems are unnecessary.
- The modular characteristic of photovoltaic energy allows arrays to be installed quickly and in any size required or allowed.
- Environmental impact of a photovoltaic system is minimal, requiring no water for system cooling and generating no by-products.
- The sitting of numerous small-scale generators in electric distribution feeders could improve the economics and reliability of the distribution system.

2.4 Construction of Photovoltaic cell

A PV cell is a p-n junction which is made from two different layers of silicon doped with a small quantity of impurity atoms: in the case of the n-layer, atoms with one more valence electron, called donors, and in the case of the p-layer, with one less valence electron, known as acceptors. In Fig. 2.1 [4], when the two layers are joined together, near the interface the free electrons of the n-layer are diffused in the p-side, leaving behind an area positively charged by the donors. Similarly, free holes in the p-layer are diffused in the n-side, leaving behind a region negatively charged by the acceptors. This creates an electrical field between the two sides that is a potential barrier to further flow. Equilibrium is reached in the junction whenelectrons and holes cannot surpass that potential barrier and consequently they cannot move. This electric field pulls the electrons and holes in opposite directions. So the current can flow in one way only:Electrons can move from the p-side to the n-side and the holes in the opposite direction.

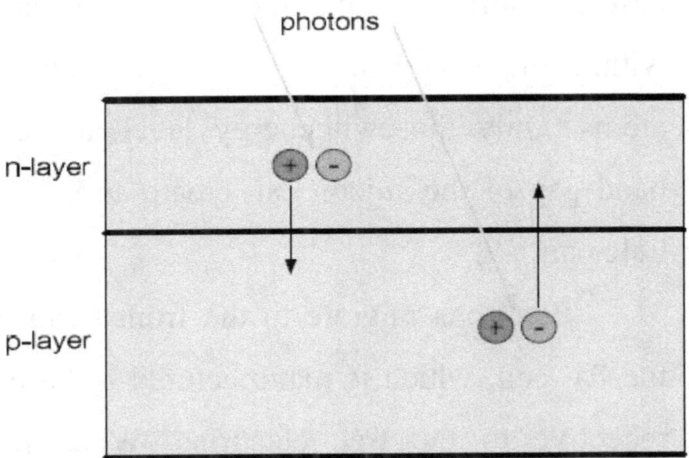

Fig.2.1.Photovoltaic cell

2.5 Working of Photovoltaic cell

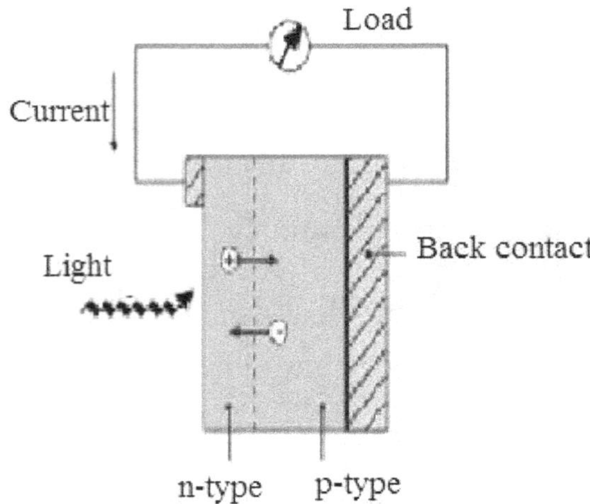

Fig.2.2. Working principle

Sunlight is composed of photons, or particles of radiant solar energy. These photons contain various amounts of energy depending on the wavelength of the solar spectrum. When the photons strike a PV cell, some are absorbed while others are reflected. When the material absorbs sufficient photon energy, electrons within the cell material dislodge from their atoms. Only thosewithenergy level above the band gap of the silicon can create an electron-hole pair.

Electrons migrate to the front surface of the PV cell, which is manufactured to be more receptive to the free electrons. When many electrons, each carrying a negative charge, travel towards the front surface of the cell, the resulting imbalance of charges between the cell's front and back surfaces creates a voltage potential like the negative and positive terminals of a battery. When the two surfaces are connected through an external load, current flows. The PV array produces direct current electricity. The light-generated current depends directly on the irradiation: if it is higher, then it contains more photons with enough energy to create more electron-hole pairs and consequently more current is generated by the PV cell.

2.6 Modelling of Photovoltaic cell

Photovoltaic cell can be represented by the electrical model shown in Fig.2.3 [4]. Its current- voltage characteristic is expressed by the following equation:

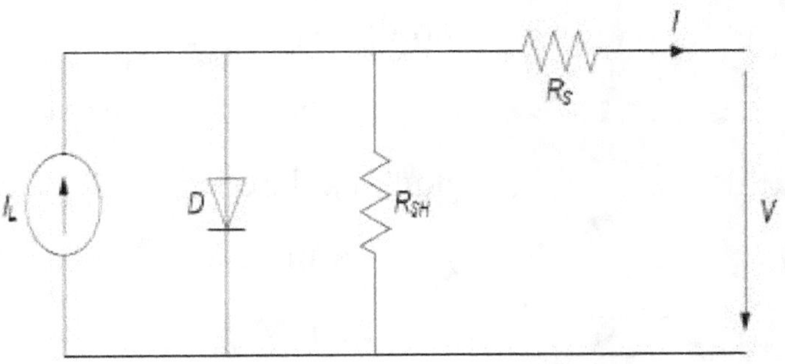

Fig.2.3. Equivalent circuit of a PV cell

$$I = I_L - I_o \left\{ e^{\frac{q(V-IR_S)}{AkT}} - 1 \right\} - \frac{V-IR_S}{R_{SH}} \quad (2.1)$$

where 'I'and 'V'are the PV cell output current and voltage respectively, 'I_o'is the darksaturation current,'q'is the charge of an electron, 'A'is the diode quality (ideality) factor, 'k'is the Boltzmann constant, 'T'is the absolute temperature and 'R_S'and 'R_{SH}'are the seriesand shunt resistances of the PV cell.

'R_S'is the resistance offered by the contacts and bulk semiconductor material of the solar cell. Shunt resistance 'R_{SH}'is related to the non ideal nature of the p–n junction andthe presence of impurities near the edges of the cell that provide a short-circuit patharound the junction. In an ideal case,'R_S'would be zero and 'R_{SH}'infinite. However, this ideal scenario is not possible and manufacturers try to minimize the effect of bothresistances to improve their products.

The effect of the shunt resistance is notconsidered, i.e. is 'R_{SH}' infinite, and so the last term is not considered in the above equation. A PV panel is composed of many cells, which are connected in series and parallel. So the output current and voltage of the PV panel are high enough to the requirements ofthe grid or equipment. Taking into account the simplification mentioned above, theoutput current-voltage characteristic of a PV panel is expressed by following equation, where 'n_p' and 'n_s'are the number of PV cells in parallel and series respectively.

$$I \approx n_p\, I_L - n_p\, I_o \left\{ e^{\frac{q(V-IR_S)}{AkTn_s}} - 1 \right\}$$

(2.2)

2.6.1 Open circuit voltage and short circuit current

Two important points of the current-voltage characteristics are: Open circuit voltage 'V_{OC}'and the short circuit current 'I_{SC}'. At both points the power generated is zero. 'V_{OC}' can be approximated from equation (2.1) when the output current of the cell is zero, i.e. $I = 0$ and the shunt resistance 'R_{SH}'is neglected. It is represented by equation (2.3). The short circuit current 'I_{SC}' is the current at $V=0$ and is approximately equal to the light generated current 'I_L'as shown in equation(2.4).

$$V_{OC} \approx \frac{AkT}{q} \ln\left\{ \frac{I_L}{I_o} + 1 \right\}$$

(2.3)

$$I_{SC} \approx I_L$$

(2.4)

Maximum power is generated by the PV cell at a point of the currentvoltagecharacteristic where the product 'VI' is maximum. This point is known as the Maximum Power Point and isunique.

2.6.2 Fill factor

Fill factor is defined as the ratio of the actual maximum power ($I_{MPP}V_{MPP}$) to the theoretical one ($I_{SC}V_{OC}$).

$$FF = \frac{I_{MPP}\,V_{MPP}}{I_{SC}V_{OC}} \qquad (2.5)$$

The MPP voltage and current are always below theopen circuit voltage and the short circuit current respectively, because of the series andshunt resistances and the diode. The typical fill factor for commercial solar cells is usually over 0.70.

2.7 Nonlinear characteristics of Photovoltaic cell

Photovoltaic cells have insolation and temperature dependent nonlinear V-I characteristics. Their operating point corresponding to maximum power changes nonlinearly with the environmental conditions (e.g., insolation, temperature and degradation levels).The main reasons for the low electrical efficiency of photovoltaic systems are the nonlinear variation of output voltage and current. Two important factors that have to be taken into account are the irradiation and the temperature. Maximum Power Point varies during the day and that is the main reason why it must constantly be tracked and ensured that the maximum available power is obtained from the PV system. Two nonlinear characteristics that can be plotted for a Photovoltaic cell are P-V and I-V characteristics, which are shown in Fig.2.4 [4].

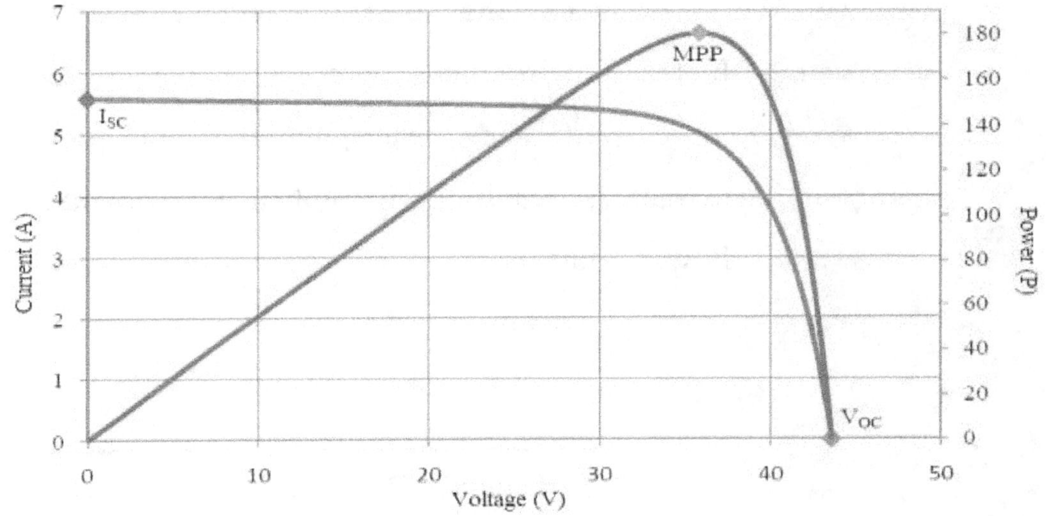

Fig.2.4. P-V & I-V characteristics

2.7.1 Effect of Irradiation

Two curves, I-V and P-V characteristics are shown in Fig.2.5 and Fig.2.6 [21]. For example, consider four levels of irradiation: 300W/ m², 500W/ m², 700W/ m², 1000W/m². The photo generated current is directly proportional to the irradiance level, so an increment in the irradiation leads to a higher photo-generated current. Moreover, the short circuit current is directly proportional to the photo generated current. Therefore, it is directly proportional to the irradiance. Hence, an increase in irradiation shifts the curves upwards. Maximum Power Point is also shifted upwards. Irradiation mainly affects the PV current. It has negligible effect on open circuit PV voltage due to logarithmic dependence of light generated current.

Hence, the overall effect is positive. Increase in irradiation causes positive increase in current and hence increase in power extracted, resulting in enhanced Maximum Power Point.

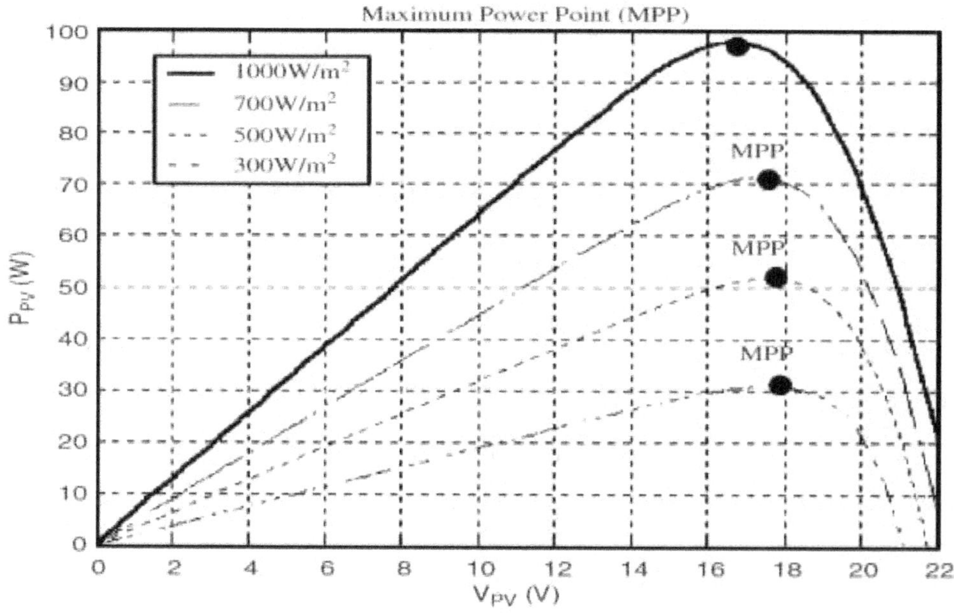

Fig. 2.5 P-V characteristics with varying irradiation.

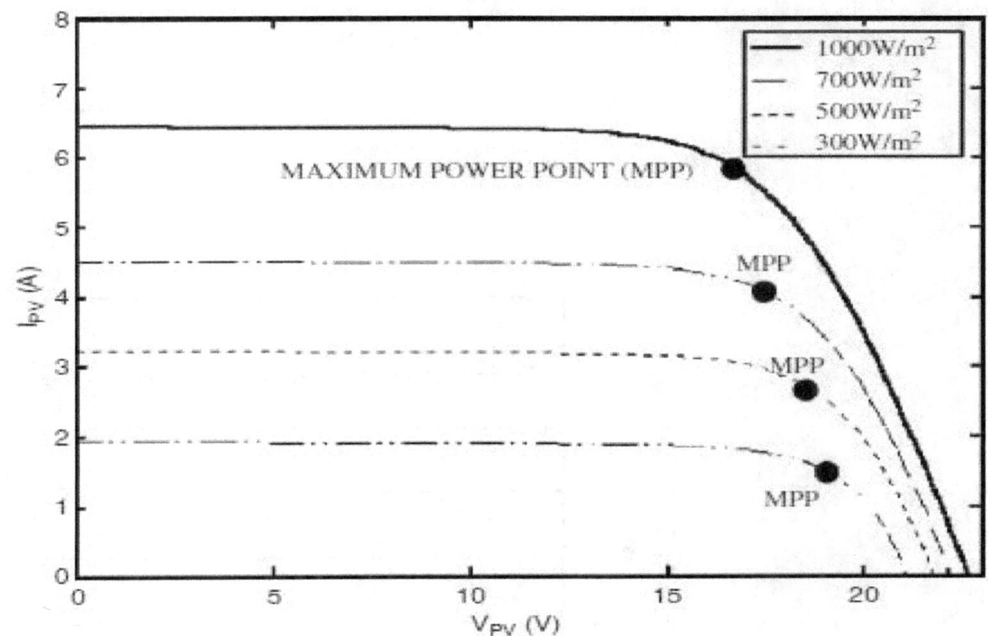

Fig.2.6. I-V characteristics with varying irradiation.

2.7.2 Effect of Temperature

Two curves, I-V and P-V characteristics are shown in Fig.2.7 and Fig.2.8 respectively [21]. Consider three temperatures 0°C, 25 °C and 50 °C. When the temperature rises, the voltage decreases. The current increaseswith the temperature but very little and it does not compensate the decrease in thevoltage caused by a given temperature rise. That is why the power also decreases.

In these figures, Maximum Power Point for 0°C is given at extreme right and for 50 °C, at extreme left, showing a decreasing trend with increase in temperature.

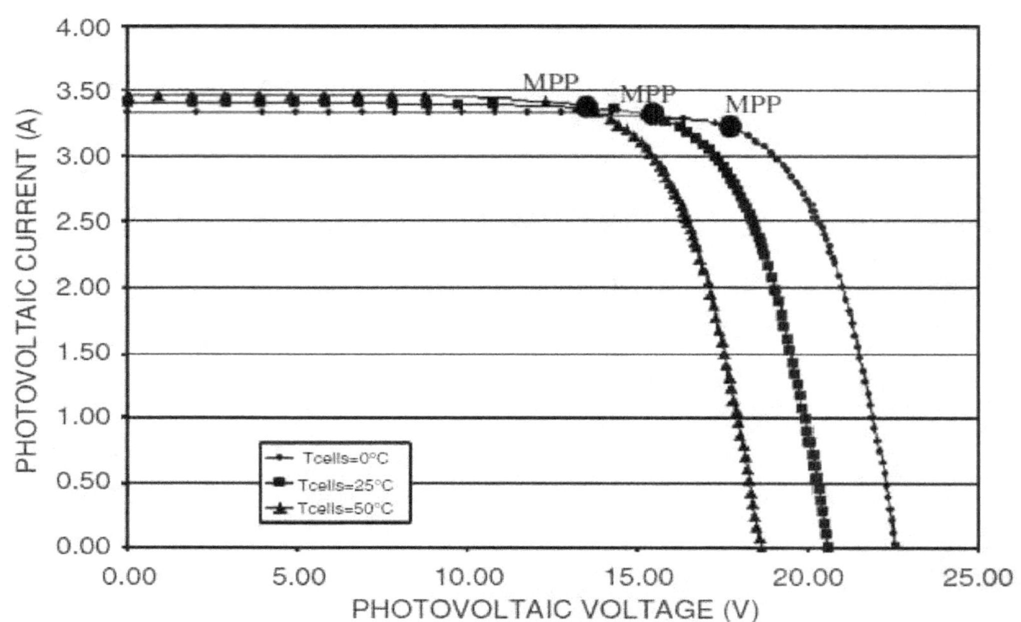

Fig. 2.7. I-V characteristics with varying temperature.

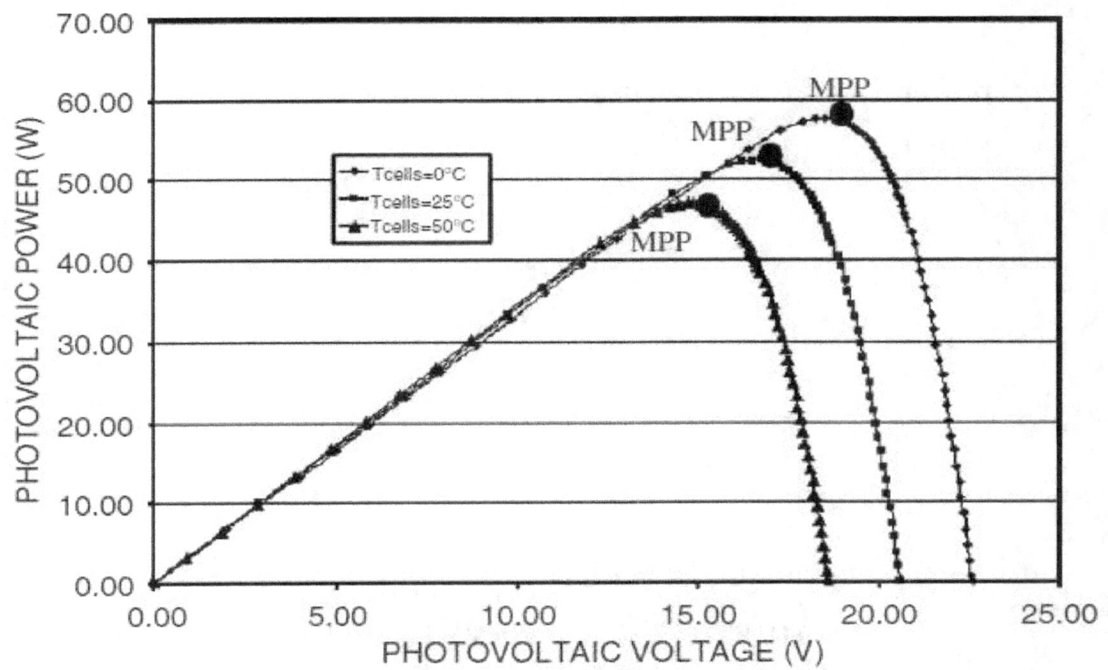

**Fig.2.8. P-V characteristics
with varying temperature**

Temperature and irradiation depend on the atmospheric conditions, which are not constant during the year and not even during a single day. They can vary rapidly due to fast changing conditions such as clouds. This causes the Maximum Power Point to move constantly, depending on the irradiation and temperature conditions. If the operating point is not close to theMaximum Power Point, great power losses occur. Hence it is essential to track the Maximum Power Pointin any condition to assure that the maximum available power is obtained from the PV panel. In a modern solar power converter, this task is entrusted to the MPPT algorithms.

CHAPTER 3
MPPT BASED PV SYSTEM

Maximum Power Point Tracking techniques are used in Photovoltaic systems to extract maximum available power under any atmospheric condition. This algorithm involves tracking the voltage at which maximum power occurs.

3.1 Maximum Power Point Tracking (MPPT)

Maximum Power Point Tracking (MPPT) is an algorithm that is included in controllers used for extracting maximum available power from PV module under certain conditions. The voltage at which PV module can produce maximum power is called 'Maximum Power Point', V_{MP}. Maximum power varies with solar radiation (sunshine & cloud), ambient temperature and cell temperature. MPPT is used to automatically find the voltage (V_{MPP})

orcurrent (I_{MPP}) at which a PV array should operate to obtain the maximum power output (P_{MPP})under a given temperature and irradiance.

3.1.1 MPPT controller

The basic principle of Maximum Power Point Tracking (MPPT) is electronic tracking. In order to get the maximum out of a PV panel, a controller should be able to choose the optimum current-voltage point on the current-voltage curve: the Maximum Power Point. An MPPT controller does exactly that. The MPPT controller is more sophisticated i.e. it will adjust its input voltage to harvest the maximum power from the PV array and then transform this power to supply the varying voltage requirement of the battery and load.

Thus, it essentially decouples the array and battery voltages so that there can be high output power. Besides performing the function of a basic controller, an MPPT controller also includes a DC to DC voltage converter, converting the voltage of the array to that required by the batteries, with very little loss of power.

3.1.2 Working of MPPT

Maximum Power Point is estimated from (a) Voltage (b) Current (c) Irradiance (d) Using empirical data (e) Mathematical expressions of numerical approximation. The estimation is carried out for a specific PV generator installed in the system. The MPPT controller is a DC to DC transformer that can transform power from a higher voltage to power at a lower voltage. The amount of power does not change (except for a small loss in the transformation process). Therefore, if the output voltage is lower than the input voltage, the output current will be higher than the input current, so that the product $P = V \times I$ remains constant.

3.1.3 Necessity of MPPT

MPPT is used to automatically find the voltage (V_{MPP}) or current (I_{MPP}) at which a PV array should operate to obtain the maximum power output (MPP) under a given temperature and irradiance. Under partial shading conditions it is possible to have multiple local maxima, but overall there is still only one true MPP. This increases the PV power which is connected to grids in large scale and small scale and also for efficient use of PV cells.

To understand more clearly how MPPT works, let us first consider the operation of a conventional controller. When a conventional controller is charging a discharged battery, it connects the modules directly to the battery.

This forces the modules to operate at battery voltage, typically not the ideal operating voltage at which the modules are able to produce their maximum available power. The PV Module Power/Voltage/Current graph shows the traditional Current/Voltage curve for a typical 75W module at standard test conditions of 25°C cell temperature and 1000W/m² of insolation. The graph shown in Fig.3.1 also shows PV module power verses module voltage curve [7].

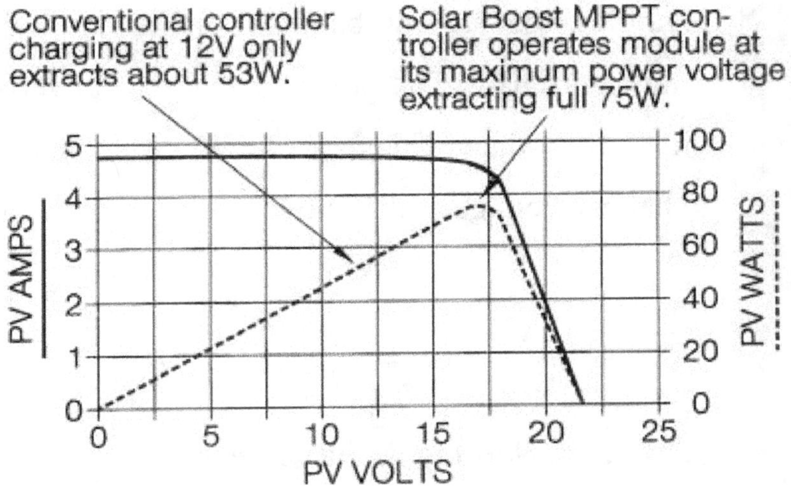

Fig.3.1. Typical 75W PV module Power/Voltage/Current at standard test conditions.

For the example shown, a conventional controller simply connects the module to the battery and therefore forces the module to operate at 12V. By forcing the 75W module to operate at 12V the conventional controller artificially limits power production to nearly 53W.

Rather than simply connecting the module to the battery, MPPT system calculates the voltage at which the module is able to produce maximum power. In this example, the maximum power voltage of the module (V_{MP}) is 17V. The MPPT system then operates the modules at 17V to extract the full 75W, regardless of present battery voltage. A high efficiency DC-to-DC power converter converts the 17V module voltage at the controller input to battery voltage at the output.

3.2 Partial shading and its causes

Partial shading on a PV panel occurs when only a part of the panel's surface is shaded. Partial shading on a panel string may occur when some panels are shaded and the others are fully illuminated. Partial shading refers to the surface of the PV array that is under shading and it can exist due to core or partial shade. Core shade and partial shade relate to the severity of the shade that hits the panels (not the surface). If the shadow casting object is situated close to the array, the panel is hit by the core shadow which reduces energy incident by approximately 60-80%.

Partial shade is brighter than core shadow and develops when greater distances are reached between the shadow casting object and the panel. The reduction of energy incident on the PV panel is about 30-40%.

For example, assume irradiance on non shaded PV cells at 1000 W/m². Core shadow effect implies irradiance values in the range of 400-200 W/m² and partial shade an irradiance value of 700 W/m2. Shading due to trees, nearby panels, tall buildings, towers, clouds, dust etc are causes of partial shading conditions.

3.2.1 Causes of power loss

Inside the solar panel, the cells are connected in series. Due to the presence ofbypass diodes, cell groups are formed, defined as the amount of cells connected anti - parallel to the same diode. Bypass diodes are there to create an alternative way for the current of the illuminated cells, when group cells cannot produce the same current (for example, when shaded). Therefore, if a cell group is shaded and the illuminated cells produce 5A, then the solar panel will produce 5A.

Power output reduction will occur but due to the short circuit on the shaded cell group and the reduction of Maximum Power Point voltage.

Solar strings are formed by PV panels that are connected in series. Series connection of the PV panels means that all panels produce the same current which is the string current. But, for the panels to produce the same current, they must be subjected to the same irradiance.

If all the panels within a string produce 5A and the shaded panel cannot conduct these 5A, the string will produce less than 5A leading to power loss. When partial shading occurs in a small surface inside a cell group (i.e. shade hits only a few solar cells from those connected to a bypass diode inside the cell) bypass diodes may not be able to protect the shaded cells. So, these PV cells are forced to operate with increased current, causing them to heat up. Constant operation under these conditions may lead to fast degradation of the shaded cells, minimizing the module's output.

The installation manual of the majority of solar panels states that partial shading should be avoided. When PV cells are under partial shading there is a mismatch of solar cell and panel characteristics. The P-V present complex multiple peaks and as a result the MPPT algorithm of the inverter cannot find the optimum operation point. There is a global maximum, but there may be many local ones. If the inverter tracks a local maximum the respective power loss can be significant, leading to poor performance for the whole system.

3.3 Block diagram of MPPT based PV system

The block diagram of MPPT based PV system is shown in Fig.3.2. The basic components are:

1. PV module
2. DC-DC boost converter
3. Controller implementing MPPT
4. Load/ Battery

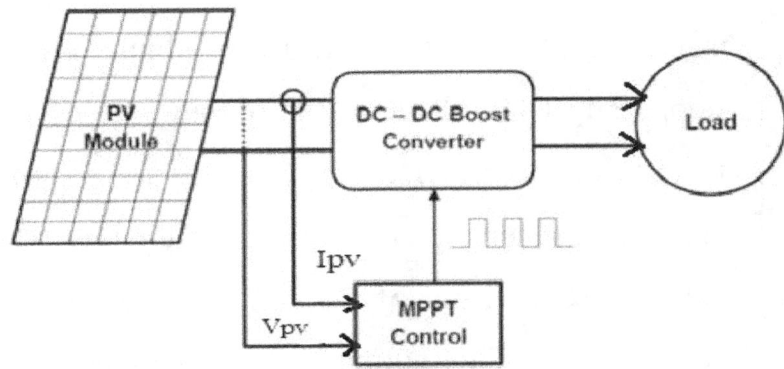

Fig.3.2. PV system with MPPT

PV module is connected to the input of boost converter. Load is connected to the output of the converter. A controller generates appropriate duty cycle based on the MPPT algorithm implemented in the system. The controller takes up PV voltage and current as inputs to generate the required duty cycle. This is used to control the gating of switches used in the converter. Thus according to variation in the environmental conditions, MPP is tracked by the controller.

3.3.1 DC-DC Boost Converter

The maximum power point tracking is basically a load matching problem. In order to change the input resistance of the panel to match the load resistance (by varying the duty cycle), a DC to DC converter is required.It basically carries out DC-DC conversion, i.e., changing one DC voltage level to another DC voltage level. The converter used in this project is a DC-DC boost converter, which gives stepped up DC voltage as the output (an output voltage greater than its input voltage). Filters made of capacitors are normally added to the output to the output of the converter to reduce voltage ripple.This output voltage is given to a load or battery. Operation of boost converter is as follows:

- When switch S is closed- Current flows through Inductor L and switch S and back to the source. The polarity of L is +ve on left side and −ve on the right side. It stores energy in the form of magnetic field.

- When switch S is open- There is reversal of polarity across the Inductor. Thus right side becomes +ve and left becomes −ve. Current, now flows through L, diode and the capacitor. Capacitor sees two sources, the first source and L in series, hence perceives voltage greater than input voltage. Hence, it gets charged to a stepped up voltage. Thus, energy stored in the L is transferred to Capacitor C.

- During the period when switch S is closed, capacitor discharges through the load because right side of the circuit is shorted out. Hence, energy is transferred to the load. Diode prevents the capacitor from discharging through the switch.

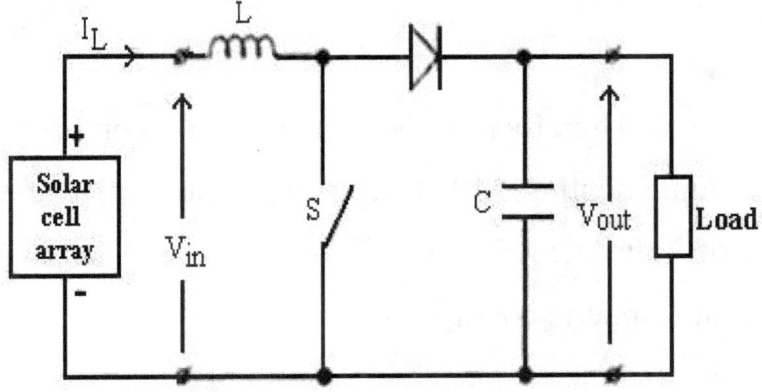

Fig.3.3. DC-DC boost converter

3.3.2 Load/ Battery

The output voltage of boost converter can be given to load or a battery. Battery is a storage unit. Load can be DC or AC load application. For AC loads, inverters are required to convert DC to AC.

3.3.3 MPPT controller

MPPT controller provides the DC-DC converter the required pulse by using MPPT algorithm and it takes PV voltage and current as inputs. This control circuit may be of any form. It implements the MPPT algorithm to increase the efficiency of PV system operation and hence helps in extracting maximum available power.

Therefore, a PV system uses a controller implementing MPPT to change the duty cycle of the converter according to varying atmospheric conditions.

CHAPTER 4
CONVENTIONAL
MPPT TECHNIQUES

Various Conventional MPPT techniques exist. Some of them are detailed below. Conventional Perturb & Observe has been described in detail.

4.1 Temperature method

Temperature method is one of the conventional methods based on the environmental conditions. The PVcell's parameters are not constant and change with the environmental condition. The cell's temperature depends on various parameters such as the case material, thermal dissipation, amount of absorption and the cell's environmental condition, e.g., ambient temperature. The output characteristic of a cell is highly nonlinear. Due to increase in the cell's temperature, as a result of reduction in the PV cell's gap, short circuit current increases approximately 0.1%. On the other hand, open circuit voltage reduces by about2 mV. Therefore, some parameters of the model are strongly related to the cell's temperature. Hence, the cell's temperature is required to predict its characteristics. This MPPT method employs temperature sensor in order to obtain a sample of the photovoltaic module surface temperature and, from it, calculates the optimal voltage to be imposed across the photovoltaic device.

4.1.1 Limitations of Temperature method

The irradiance or temperature sensors are very expensive and uncommon.

4.2 Constant Voltage method (CV)

The Constant Voltage (CV) algorithm is the simplest MPPT control method. The operating point of the PV array is, each nth step, kept near the Maximum Power Point by regulating the array voltage and matching it to a fixed reference voltage V_{REF} equal to the V_{MPP} of the characteristic PV module or another prevaluated best voltage value. The CV method needs the measurement of the PV array voltage in order to set up the duty-cycle of the DC/DC boost converter. It is important that when the

PV panel is in low insulation conditions, the CV technique is, generally, more effective than either the P&O method or the InC method.

4.2.1 Limitations of CV method

The CV method assumes that insulation and temperature variations on the array are insignificant on the V_{MPP}, and that the constant reference voltage V_{REF} is an adequate approximation of the real MPP. Therefore, the operating point is never exactly at the MPP and different data have to be adopted for different geographical regions.

4.3 Fractional Short Circuit Current(SC)

It is required to periodically short the PV array so that I_{SC} can be measured using a current sensor. The optimum operating current for maximum output power is proportional to the short circuit current I_{SC} under various conditions of irradiance level. The SC method needs the measurement of the PV array current (I_{PV}) linearly related to the I_{SC} of the PV array in order to set up the duty-cycle of the DC/DC boost converter.

4.3.1 Limitations of SC method

This method requires an additional static switch, yet they provide low energy supply. It does not follow the instantaneous time trend, because change in irradiance causes change in step size between two consecutive electronic switching. This method cannot calculate the new Maximum Power Point, until the new level of solar insulation is measured. It is an approximate method.

4.4 Fractional Open Circuit Voltage (FOCV)

The near linear relationship between V_{MPP} and V_{OC} of the PV array, under varying irradiance and temperature levels, has given rise to the FOCV method. V_{MPP} can be computed with V_{OC} measured periodically by momentarily shutting down the power converter. It is necessary to introduce a static switch into the PV system to open the circuit for the FOCV method.

4.4.1 Limitations of FOCV method

This method causes temporary loss of power. It does not follow the instantaneous time trend. These techniques cannot calculate the newMaximum Power Point, until the new level of solar insulation is measured. It is an approximate method.

4.5 Sliding Mode Control

Sliding Mode Control is a powerful and nonlinear control technique. The sliding mode controller drives the system state to a 'custom-built' sliding (switching) surface and constrains the state to this surface thereafter. A system motion on a sliding surface, named a sliding mode, is robust with respect to matched disturbances and uncertainties but may be sensitive to unmatched ones. It is a current-based technique. The sensing of current in the capacitor placed in parallel with the photovoltaic source is one of the innovative aspects of this technique. A dual control loop based on the sliding mode control ensures a very fast tracking of irradiation variations.

4.5.1 Limitations of Sliding Mode Control

As the maximum power point of a photovoltaic (PV) cell varies mainly with incident illumination and ambient temperature, the PV cell may generate a wide range of voltages and currents at the terminals. As a consequence, the PV cell itself cannot maintain a constant DC voltage and function as a DC voltage power supply source.

4.6 Differential Method

In this method, there are many equations to be solved very quickly in order to provide accurate operating point. Comparison of Ipv.dVpv+Vpv.dIpv to an equal perturbation on the opposite side of the operating point or the operating point power is required.

4.6.1 Limitations of Differential method

The limitation of this method is that it requires more calculation time. This is done till final sum becomes zero, if not than more calculations are required.

4.7 Curve fitting method

The Curve-fitting method is an offline method where PV module characteristics, data and manufacturing details are required. Mathematical model and equations describing the output characteristics are pre-decided.

4.7.1 Limitations of Curve fitting method

The limitation of Curve fitting method is that it requires prior and accurate knowledge of physical parameters. It requires large memory as number of calculation is more and speed is less.

4.8 Look up table method

In this method, the measured values of the PV generator's voltage and current are compared with those stored in the control system, which correspond to the operation in the maximum point, under concrete climatological conditions.

4.8.1 Limitations of Look up table method

The limitation is that a large capacity of memory is required for storage of the data. Also, it is required that the implementation should be adjusted for a specific panel PV. In addition, it is difficult to record and store all possible system conditions.

4.9 Incremental conductance method

The Incremental Conductance (InC) algorithm was developed to overcome drawbacks of other conventional methods under rapidly changing weather conditions. In incremental conductance method the array terminal voltage is always adjusted according to the Maximum Power Point voltage. It is based on the incremental and instantaneous conductance of the PV module.

This method exploits the assumption that the ratio of change in output conductance is equal to the negative output Instantaneous conductance i.e. the PV module operates at its Maximum Power Point when the InC dI/dV is equal to its direct conductance -I/V. While, if the PV module dI/dV is greater than the its conductance -I/V, then the controller would increase the PV module voltage by adjusting the duty ratio of a DC –DC converter, otherwise, the perturbation would be in the opposite direction or to increase the duty ratio of the converter in order to reduce the voltage and shift the operating point back to the Maximum Power Point.

4.9.1 Limitation of Incremental Conductance method

The limitation of InC is that it requires complex control circuits.

4.10 Fuzzy Logic Algorithm

Microcontrollers have made using fuzzy logic control popular for MPPT over the last decade. Fuzzy logic controllers have the advantages of working with imprecise inputs, not needing an accurate mathematical model, and handling nonlinearity. Fuzzy logic was developed to address uncertainty and imprecision which widely exist in the engineering problems for solving power system problems.

Fuzzy set theory can be considered as a generation of the classical set theory. In classical set theory an element of the universe either belongs to or does not belong to the set. Thus, the degree of associations of an element is crisp. In a fuzzy set theory the association of an element can be continuously varying.

Mathematically, a fuzzy set is a mapping (known as membership function) from the universe of discourse to the closed interval. The membership function is usually designed by taking into consideration the requirement and constraints of the problem. Fuzzy logic implements human experiences and preferences via membership functions and fuzzy rules.

4.10.1 Limitations of Fuzzy Logic method

Many localized parameters are used. In areas that have good mathematical descriptions and solutions, the use of fuzzy logic most often may be sensible when computing power.

4.11 Conventional Perturb and Observe (P&O)

The following section describes the Conventional P&O method in detail.

4.11.1 Introduction

The P&O algorithm is also called "hill-climbing", but both names refer to the same algorithm depending on how it is implemented. In the case of a PV system connected to a power converter, perturbing the duty ratio of power converter perturbs the PV system current, and consequently perturbs the PV system voltage. P&O involves a perturbation in the operating voltage of the DC link between the PV and the power converter. The Perturb and Observe (P&O) algorithm is the most commonly used in practice because of fewer measured parameters and ease of implementation in its basic form. P&O is an iterative method.

4.11.2 Overview of Conventional P&O

In the P&O algorithm, the operating voltage of the PV system is perturbed by a small increment, and the resulting change in power, ΔP, is measured. If ΔP is positive, then the perturbation of the operating voltage moves the PV system's operating point closer to the Maximum Power Point (MPP). Thus, further voltage perturbations in the same direction (that is, with the same algebraic sign) should move the operating point toward the Maximum Power Point.

If ΔP is negative, the system operating point has moved away from the MPP, and the algebraic sign of the perturbation should be reversed to move back towards the MPP. Thus,if the magnitude of power is increasing, the perturbation will continue in the same direction in the next cycle, otherwise the perturbation direction is reversed.

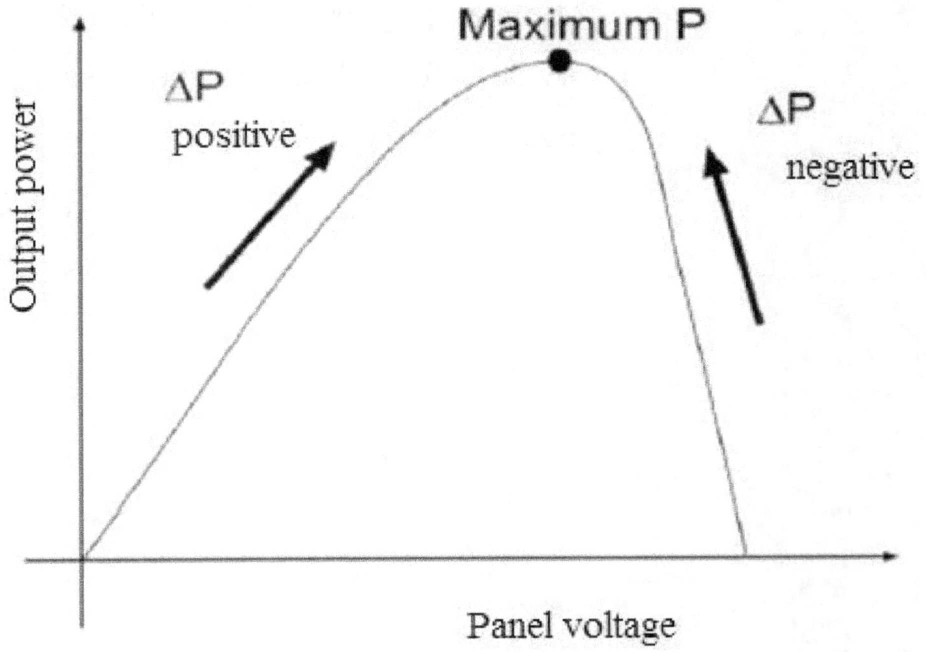

Fig.4.1. P-V curve

The above figure shows the variation of output power with PV system voltage. It shows that the change in power is positive when moving from left side of the graph to right and it is negative when moving from right side to the left. This change in power affects the direction of perturbation of the operating voltage during every cycle.

Flow chart for this technique is shown in Fig.4.2. This flowchart shows that there is change in the duty cycle of the converter to track the Maximum Power

4.11.3 Advantages of Conventional P&O

The advantages of conventional P&O are

1. This method is relatively simple.
2. The time complexity of this algorithm is very less for calculating the maximum power.

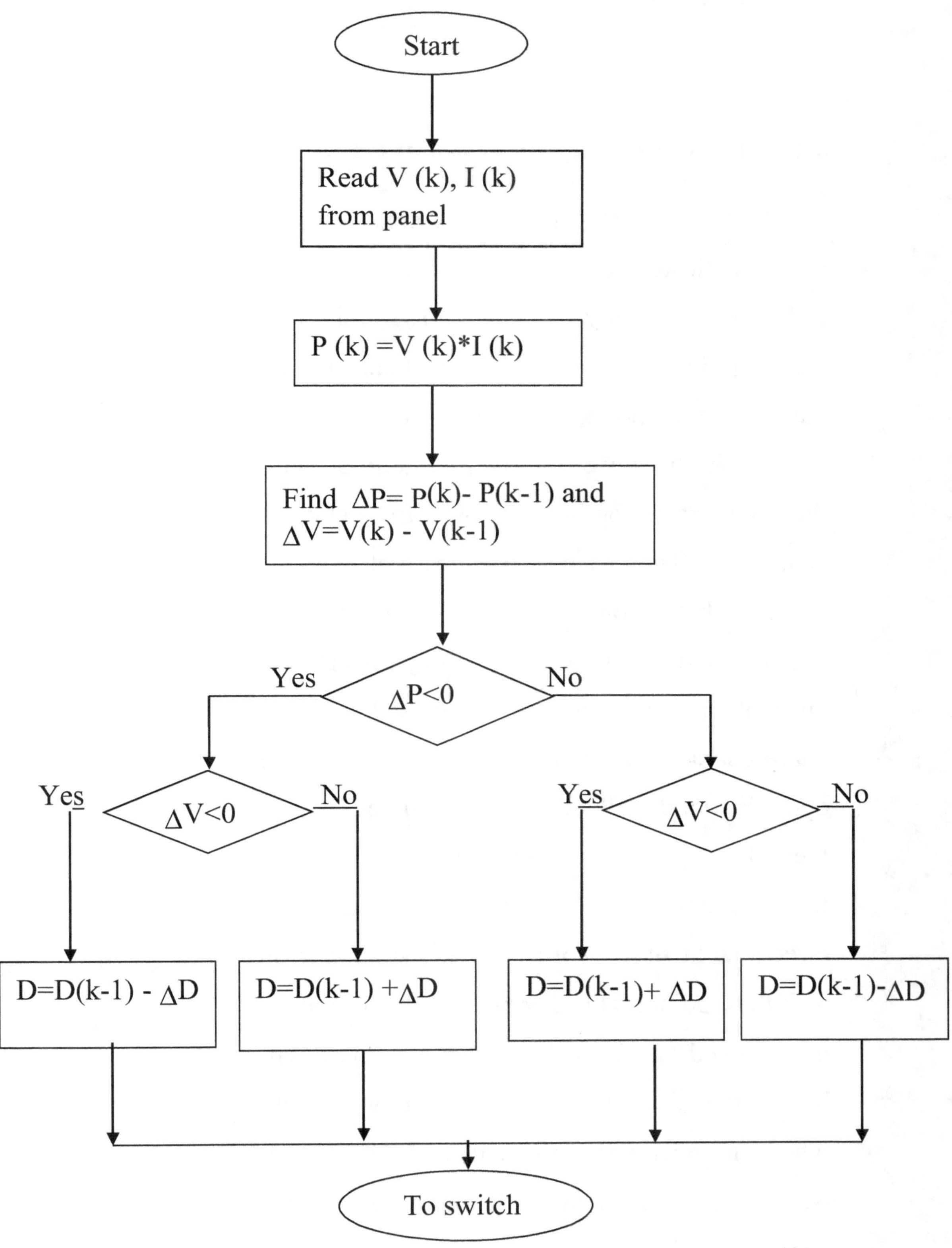

Fig.4.2 Flow chart for P&O

4.11.4 Limitations of Conventional P&O

In Fig.4.3 [21], the case is considered in which the irradiance is such that it generates the P–V curve characteristics, curve 1. In this way, the operating voltage initially oscillates around the maximum point, from A to A1. Now, an increase in the power will be measured because the solar irradiation has increased from curve 1 to curve 2. Then, if one assumes that being in point A, that it comes from a diminution of the voltage, and before the following disturbance takes place, the irradiance is increased, with the curve characteristic being now curve 2, and the operationpoint will occur at B1. Indeed, since there has been a positive increase in power, thedisturbance will continue in the same direction. In other words, voltagewill diminish and go to point B. Furthermore, if the irradiance is increased again quickly tocurve 3, there will be another increase in positive power, with which the operation point will now be C. That is, due to two increases of irradiance, the operation point has been transferred from A to C, moving away from the maximum point. This process remains until the increase of the irradiance slows or stops.

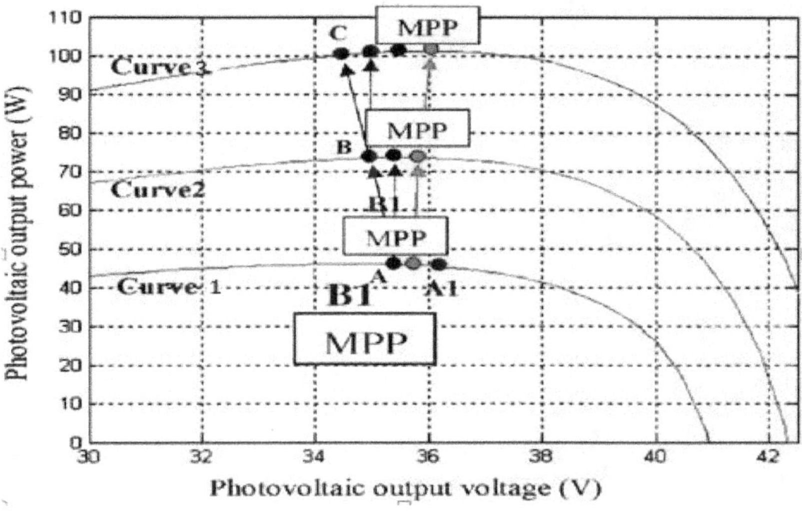

Fig.4.3 Deviation from MPP under varying irradiance

The disadvantages are as follows:

1. Once the MPP is reached, there are many oscillations around this point.

2. It is a trial and error process.

3. The system may fail to track the MPP under varying atmospheric conditions.

4. Under varying atmospheric conditions, there may be several peaks and the algorithm may not be able to track the true peak.

5. It is a slow method to find the Maximum Power Point.

Thus, the conventional MPPT techniques are presented. Conventional P&O method has been described in detail.

CHAPTER 5
OPTIMIZATION TECHNIQUES

Optimization techniques such as Artificial Neural networks (ANN), Ant colony optimization (ACO), Genetic Algorithm (GA) and Particle Swarm Optimization (PSO) are detailed below.

5.1 Artificial Neural networks (ANN)

An artificial neural network (ANN) is a computational device that consists of many simple connected units (neurons) that work in parallel. The connections between the units or nodes are usually weighted by real-valued weights. Weights are the primary means of learning in neural networks, and a learning algorithm is usually used to adjust the weights. An artificial neural network is a parallel distribution of linear processing units arranged as layers. Parallelism, modularity and dynamic adaptation are computational characteristics associated with networks. These characteristics support FPGA implementation of networks, because parallelism takes advantage of FPGA concurrency, and modularity and dynamic adaptation benefit from network reconfiguration. The most important aspects of FPGA implementation of neural networks are the benefits of reconfiguration, the representation of internal data and implementation issues like weight precision and transfer functions.

5.2 Ant colony optimization (ACO)

It is a probabilistic technique. Searching for optimal path in the graph based on behaviour of ants seeking a path between their colony and source of food. It is a heuristic method for solving a very general class of computational problems by combining user-given heuristics in the hope of obtaining a more efficient procedure.Soft computing technique for solving hard discrete optimization problems. Artificial Intelligence technique used to develop a new method to solve problems unsolvable since last many years. Artificial ants implement a randomized construction heuristic which makes probabilistic decisions ACO shows great performance with the "ill-structured" problems like network routing.

5.3 Genetic Algorithm (GA)

The basic binary encoded Genetic Algorithm (GA) employs tournament selection, uniform crossover and low probability mutation rate is employed to solve the benchmark problems and the space systems design problems. The GA

represents the design variables of each individual design with binary strings of 0's and 1's that are referred to as chromosomes. It is important to note that the GA works with a coding for the design parameters that allows for a combination of discrete and continuous parameters in one problem statement. This encoding feature also forces the design variables to only take values that are within their upper and lower bounds, i.e., no solutions will ever violate the side constraints and infeasibility can only occur because of violation of functional constraints. The GA begins its search from a randomly generated population of designs that evolve over successive generations (iterations), eliminating the need for a user-supplied starting point. To perform its optimization-like process, the GA employs three operators to propagate its population from one generation to another. The first operator is the

"Selection" operator that mimics the principal of "Survival of the Fittest". The second operator is the "Crossover" operator, which mimics mating in biological populations. The crossover operator propagates features of good surviving designs from the current population into the future population, which will have better fitness value on average. The last operator is "Mutation", which promotes diversity in population characteristics. The mutation operator allows for global search of the design space and prevents the algorithm from getting trapped in local minima.

5.4 Particle Swarm Optimization (PSO)

The following section describes Particle Swarm Optimization (PSO) in detail.

5.4.1 Introduction

The particle swarm optimization (PSO) algorithm is a population-based optimization algorithm inspired by the social behaviour of bird flocking and fish schooling where each individual is referred to as particle and represents a candidate solution.This method has been inspired by the behaviour of a class of birds, in which a number of particles are used that constitute a group and move in search space to find the best solution.

5.4.2 Overview of PSO

In PSO, the potential solutions, called particle, fly through the problem space by following the current optimum particles. PSO uses several cooperative agents (particles) and each agent shares the information attained by each individual during the search process.An important element of PSO is that the members of the population "interact", or "influence" each other. Here PSO initializes the variables randomly in a given space. The number of decision variables determines the dimension of space. Each optimization problem is to search the solution space of a particle, each particle runs at a certain speed in the search space, the speed of particles is in accordance with its own flight experience and flight experience of other particles. In the optimization space, each particle has decided to adapt the objective function value, and recorded their own best position 'Pi' found so far, and the entire group of all particles found in the best position 'Pg'. In PSO, each particle tries to improve itself by imitating traits from their successful peers.The particles change its condition according to the following three principles: (1) to keep its inertia (2) to change the condition according to its most optimist position (3) to change the condition according to the swarm's most optimist position. Each particle is given with two vectors of position and velocity.The general formula used is

$$x_{ki+1} = x_{ki} + v_{ki+1} \quad (5.1)$$

$$v_{ki+1} = w * v_{ki} + c_1 r_1$$

$$(p_{ki} - x_{ki}) + c_2 r_2 (p_{kg} - x_{ki}$$

$$)(5.2) \text{ where}$$

$x_k{}^i$ - Particle position

$v_k{}^i$ - Particle velocity

$p_k{}^i$ - Best "remembered" individual particle position

$p_k{}^g$ - Best "remembered" swarm position

c_1, c_2 - learning parameters

r_1, r_2 - Random numbers between 0 and 1

w - Weight inertia

5.4.3 Algorithm

The general algorithm used for PSO is as follows:

Step 1: Start the process.

Step 2: Generate the initial population randomly by using random initialization of variables. Set the population, iterations etc.

Step 3: Evaluate the fitness value of every particle.

Step 4: Determine the best positions of the particle and also the global best. Step 5: Update the velocity and position of each particle according to the above given equation.

Step 6: Continue until maximum iterations or convergence condition.

Step 7: Result obtained in this step is the optimum solution.

General flow chart for this algorithm is as follows:

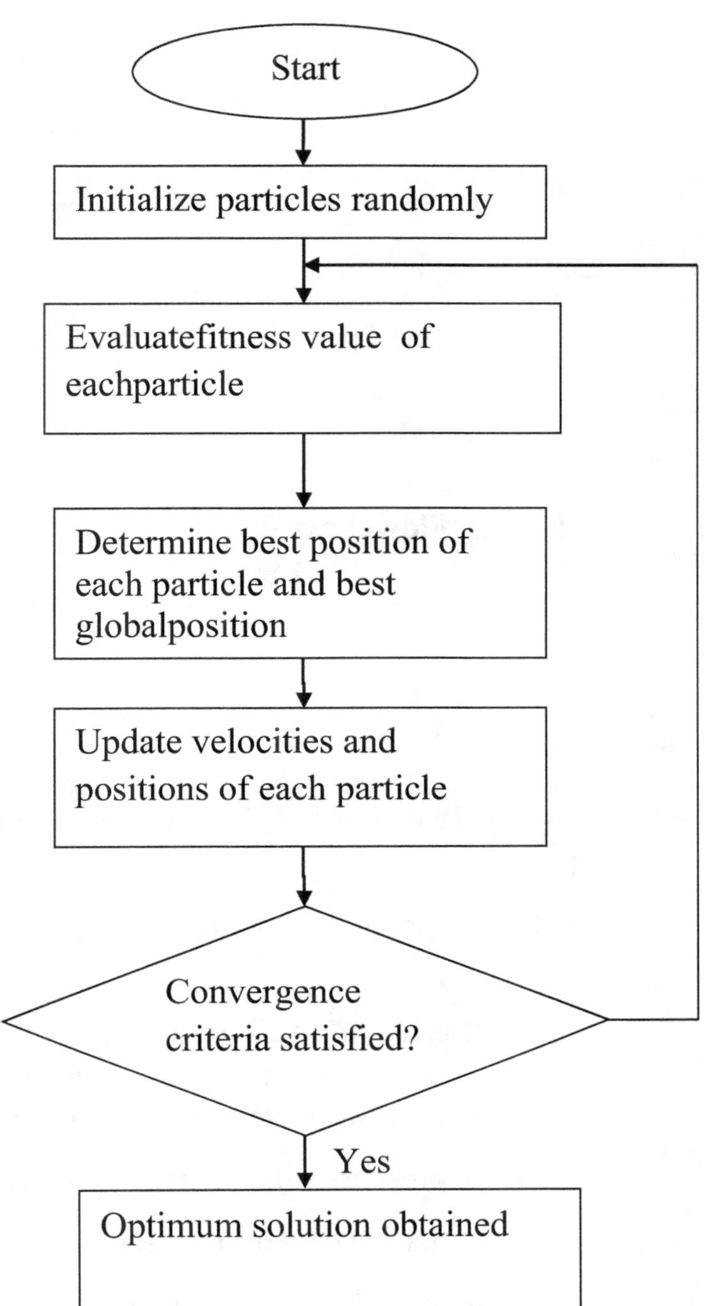

Start
Initialize particles randomly
Evaluatefitness value of eachparticle
Determine best position of each particle and best globalposition
Update velocities and positions of each particle
Convergence criteria satisfied?
Yes
Optimum solution obtained
No

Fig.5.1 Flowchart for PSO

5.4.4 Advantages of PSO over conventional P&O

The advantages of PSO over conventional P&O are

1. It is an optimization process.
2. It is faster than P&O; hence settles to final result faster, with less time delay.
3. It presents almost negligible oscillations under varying atmospheric conditions.
4. It can be used under partial shading conditions.
5. Its tracking efficiency is higher.
6. Its convergence speed is fast.
7. It can be used in conditions of many local maxima to find the global maxima.

Therefore, various optimization techniques have been presented and PSO has been detailed.

Flow chart, algorithm and advantages of PSO have been given.

CHAPTER 6

SIMULATION OF MPPT BASED PV SYSTEM

MATLAB/SIMULINK models of MPPT based PV system have been done which implement Conventional P&O and PSO. A comparison of the two techniques has also been presented based on simulation results.

6.1 MATLAB/SIMULINK

MATLAB stands for MATrix LABoratory. MATLAB was written originally to provide easy access to matrix software developed by the LINPACK (linear system package) and EISPACK (Eigen system package) projects. MATLAB is a high-performance language for technical computing. It integrates computation, visualization, and programming environment.

MATLAB is a modern programming language environment: it has sophisticated data structures, contains built-in editing and debugging tools, and supports object-oriented programming. These factors make MATLAB an excellent tool used for teaching and research.

Simulink is a block diagram environment for multi domain simulation and Model-Based Design. It is integrated with MATLAB, enabling to incorporate MATLAB algorithms into models and export simulation results to MATLAB for further analysis.

Simulink provides a graphical editor for building models as block diagrams, allowing to draw models similar to using pencil and paper. Simulink also includes a comprehensive library of sink, source, linear and nonlinear component, and connector blocks.

If these blocks do not meet needs, however, provision is there to create own blocks. The interactive environment simplifies the modeling process, eliminating the need to formulate differential and difference equations in a language or program.

6.2 Simulation model of MPPT based PV systems

MATLAB/SIMULINK models have been built to simulate the performance of conventional P&O and PSO algorithms. A comparison has also been made between the two techniques. Elements of the model are the following:

1. PV model

2. Controlled current source

3. DC-DC boost converter circuit (L, C, IGBT switch, Diode)

4. MPPT controller block- P&O

5. Delay unit at the output of controller block

6. Voltage and Current measurement blocks (VM_1, VM_2, and CM_3)

6.2.1 PV model

A PV model has been built, which takes two inputs, Temperature 'T' and Irradiation 'S'. It is modeled as a current source. Its output is current 'I', which is given to the Controlled current source block. Across this, Voltage of the PV model is measured using VM_1.

This voltage 'V' is given to PV model as feedback to enhance effectively, the working of PV subsystem. Constant temperature of 25°C and irradiation of 400 W/m² are set in the PV model. Fig. 6.2 shows the PV model. It shows the PV subsystem.

6.2.2 DC-DC boost converter

DC-DC boost converter is modeled as shown in Fig. 6.1. It is modeled using L, C, IGBT switch and diode. The gate signal of IGBT switch is controlled by MPPT controller. Duty cycle is controlled by an MPPT algorithm.

The duty cycle is given to gate via a delay block. The output of boost converter is the boosted voltage (stepped up). This voltage is measured using VM_2. The current output is measured using CM_3. This output voltage is viewed using scope.

6.2.3 MPPT Controller

This controller block implements an MPPT algorithm for controlling the duty cycle of converter. It has four inputs and one output. Inputs: Enable MPPT, MPPT parameters, V (PV model voltage), I (PV model output current) .It has one output which is the duty cycle, D.

- Enable MPPT: It is a signal used to enable MPPT. It outputs a step.
- MPPT parameters: Four parameters have been considered:
  - Amount of radiation
  - Constant current
  - Temperature

➤ Shadow conditions

- V: The voltage generated by PV model is given as input to controller.
- I: Output current of PV model is given as input.
- Duty cycle, D: The MPPT algorithm acts on the duty cycle. This is given to the gate of IGBT. This is use for switching IGBT accordingly.

6.2.4 Display using Scope

Boosted voltage from VM_2 is given to the scope to view the output waveform. Scope is used to view waveforms in MATLAB/SIMULINK. Number of parameter for which waveforms are required can be set according to the requirement. Using multiplexer, waveforms for 2 or more parameters can be obtained in the same graph. This can be used for comparison of parameters.

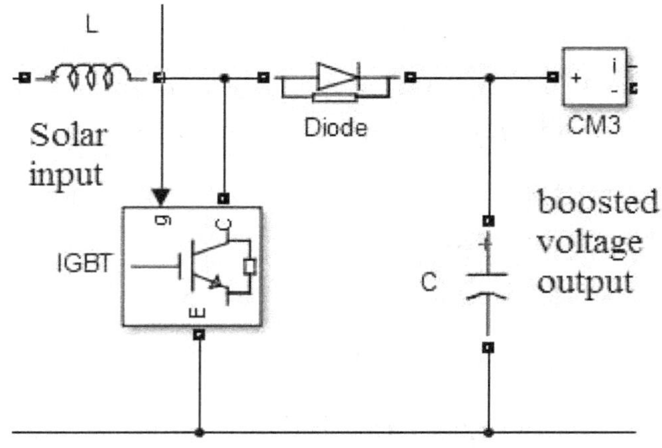

Fig. 6.1 DC-DC boost converter model

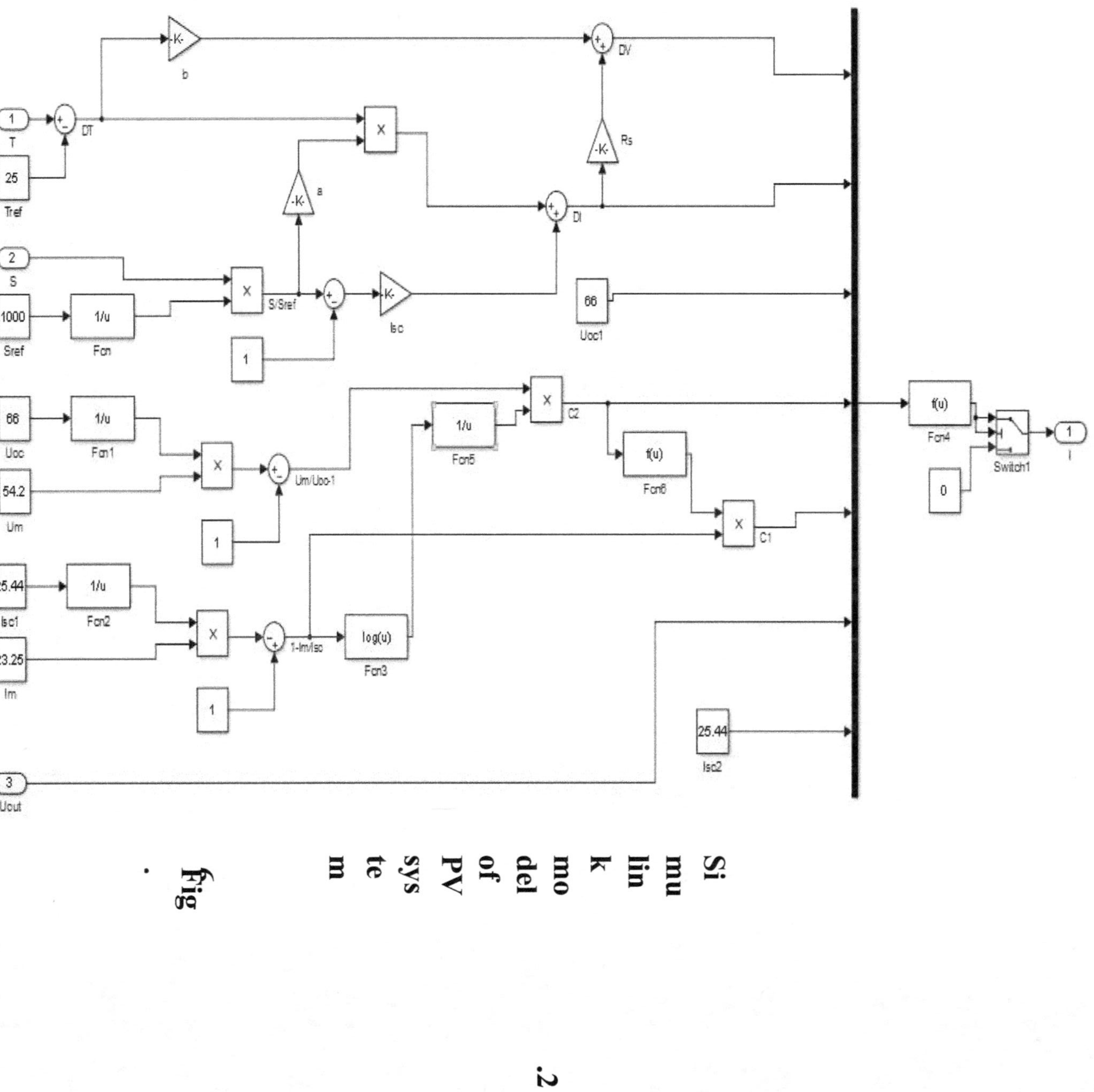

Fig. 6.2 Simulink model of PV system

Model used to simulate the performance of conventional P&O is shown in Fig.6.3

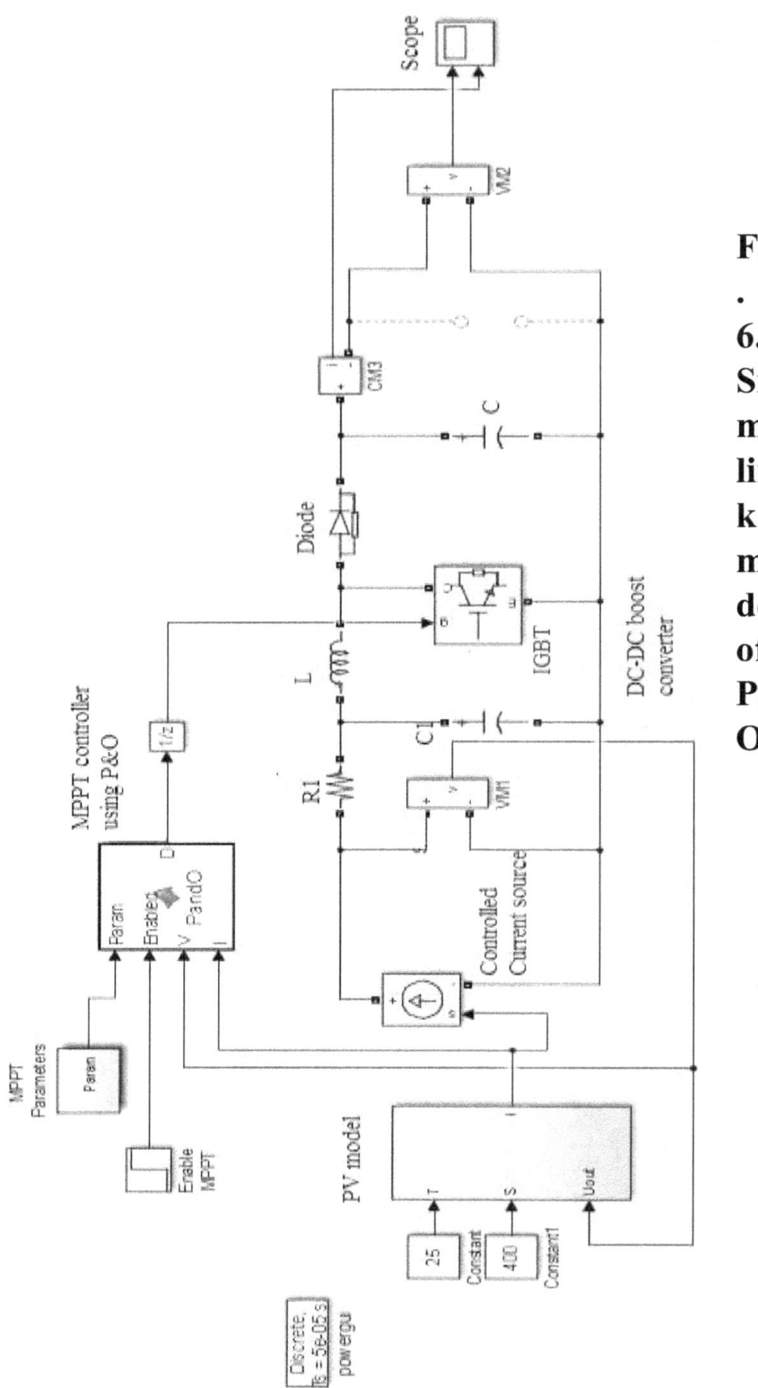

Fig. 6.3 Simulink model of P&O

Model used to simulate the performance of PSO is shown in Fig. 6.4.

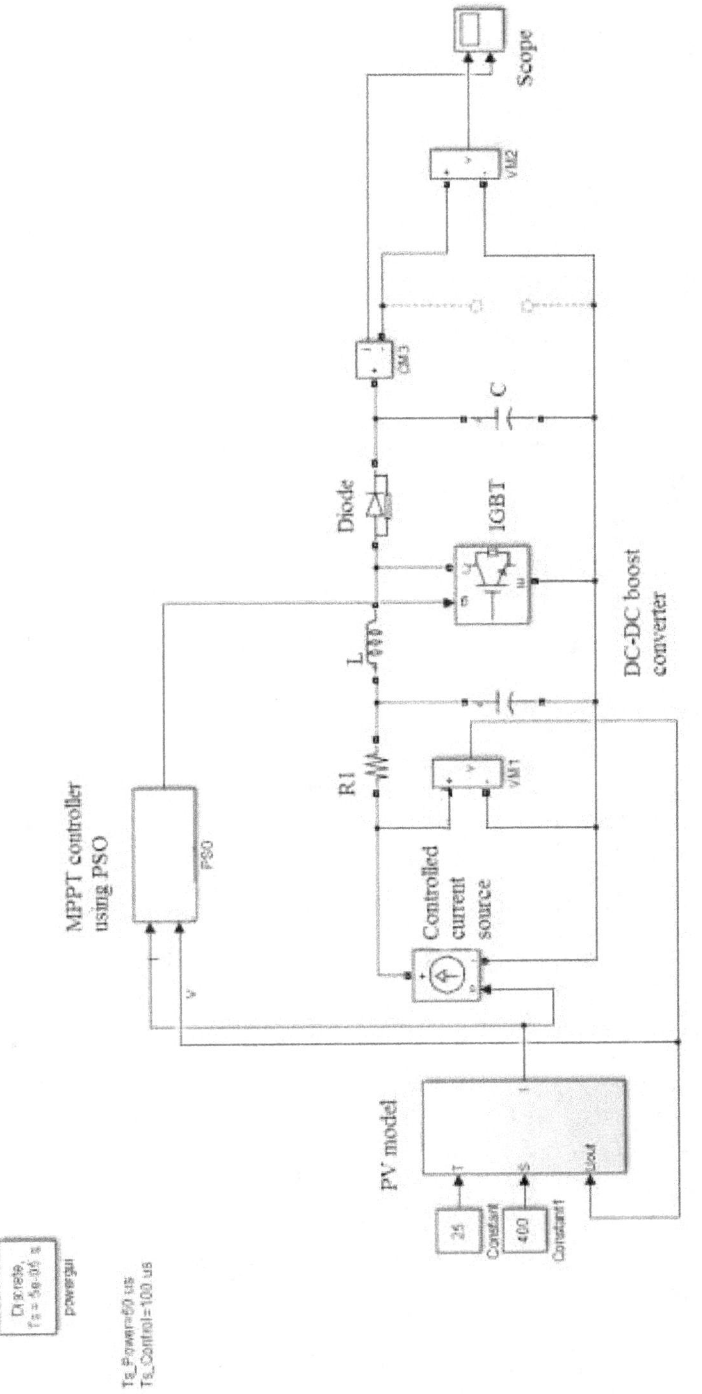

Fig. 6.4 Simulink model of PSO

Model used to simulate the comparison of conventional P&O and PSO is shown in Fig. 6.5

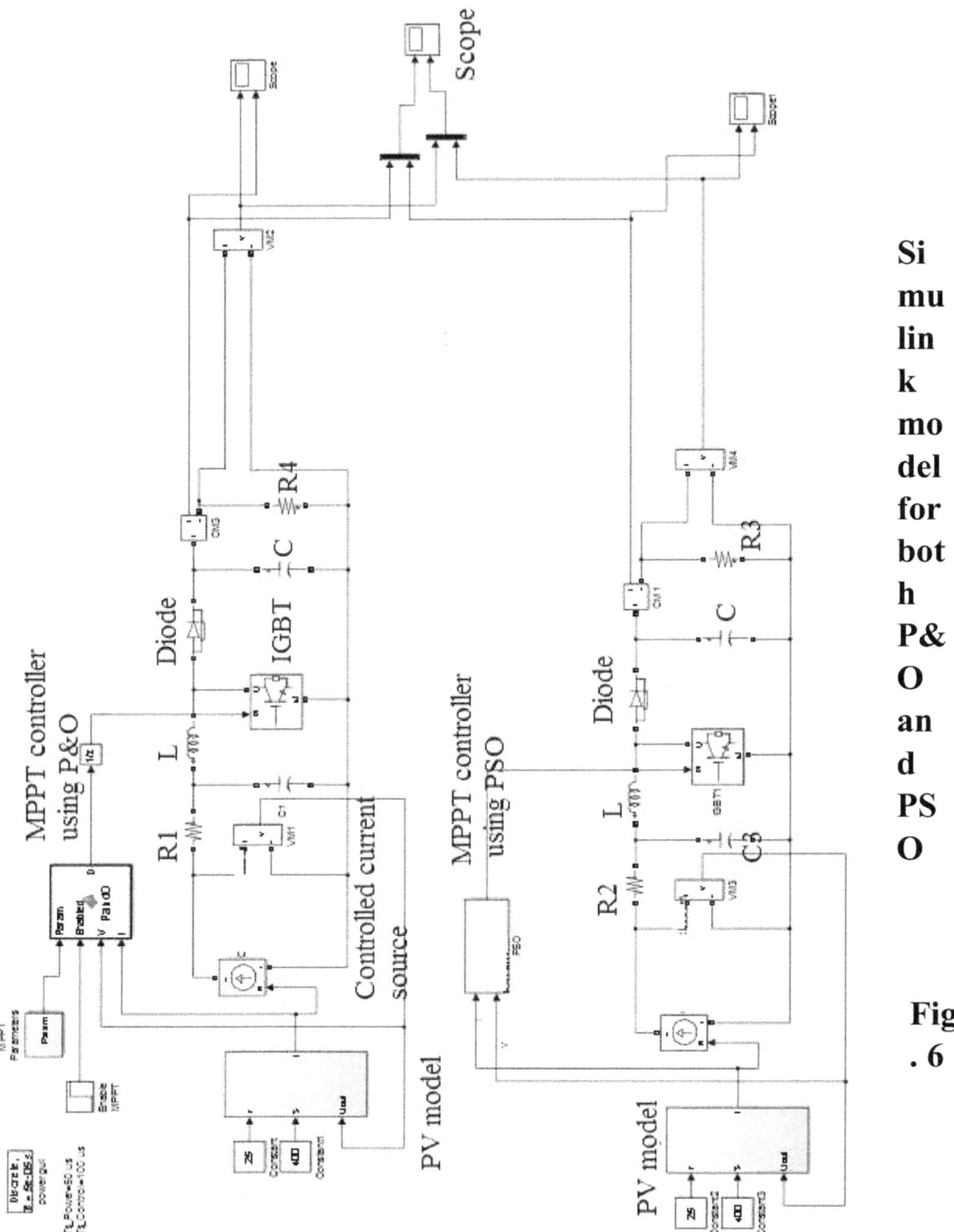

Fig. 6.5 Simulink model for both P&O and PSO

6.3 Simulation results for Conventional P&O

Fig.6.6 shows the output waveform for conventional P&O. The inference is given below.

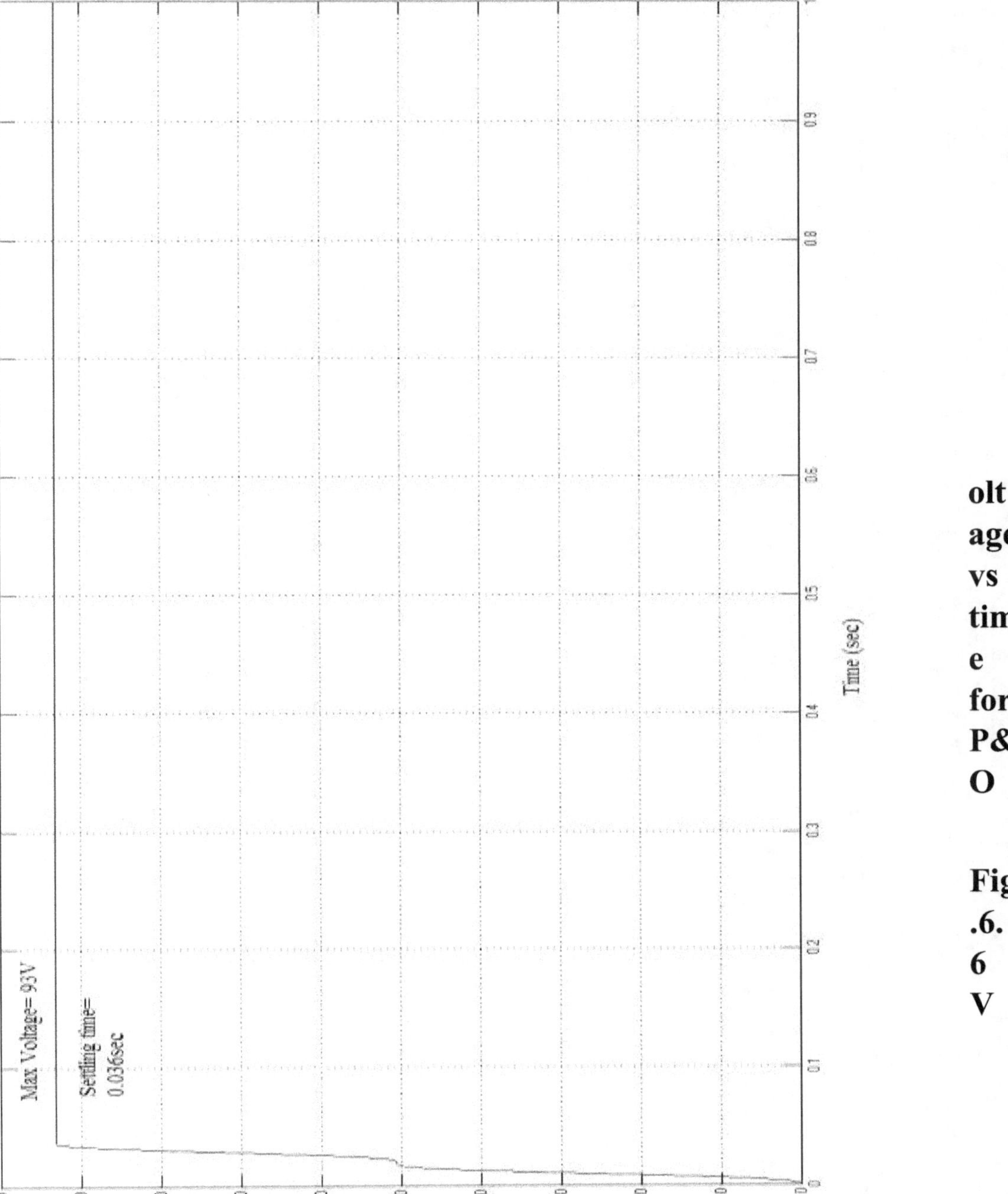

Fig.6.6 Voltage vs time for P&O

Output voltage = 93V, Settling time= 0.036 sec.

6.4 Simulation results for PSO

Fig.6.7 shows the output waveform for PSO. The inference is given below.

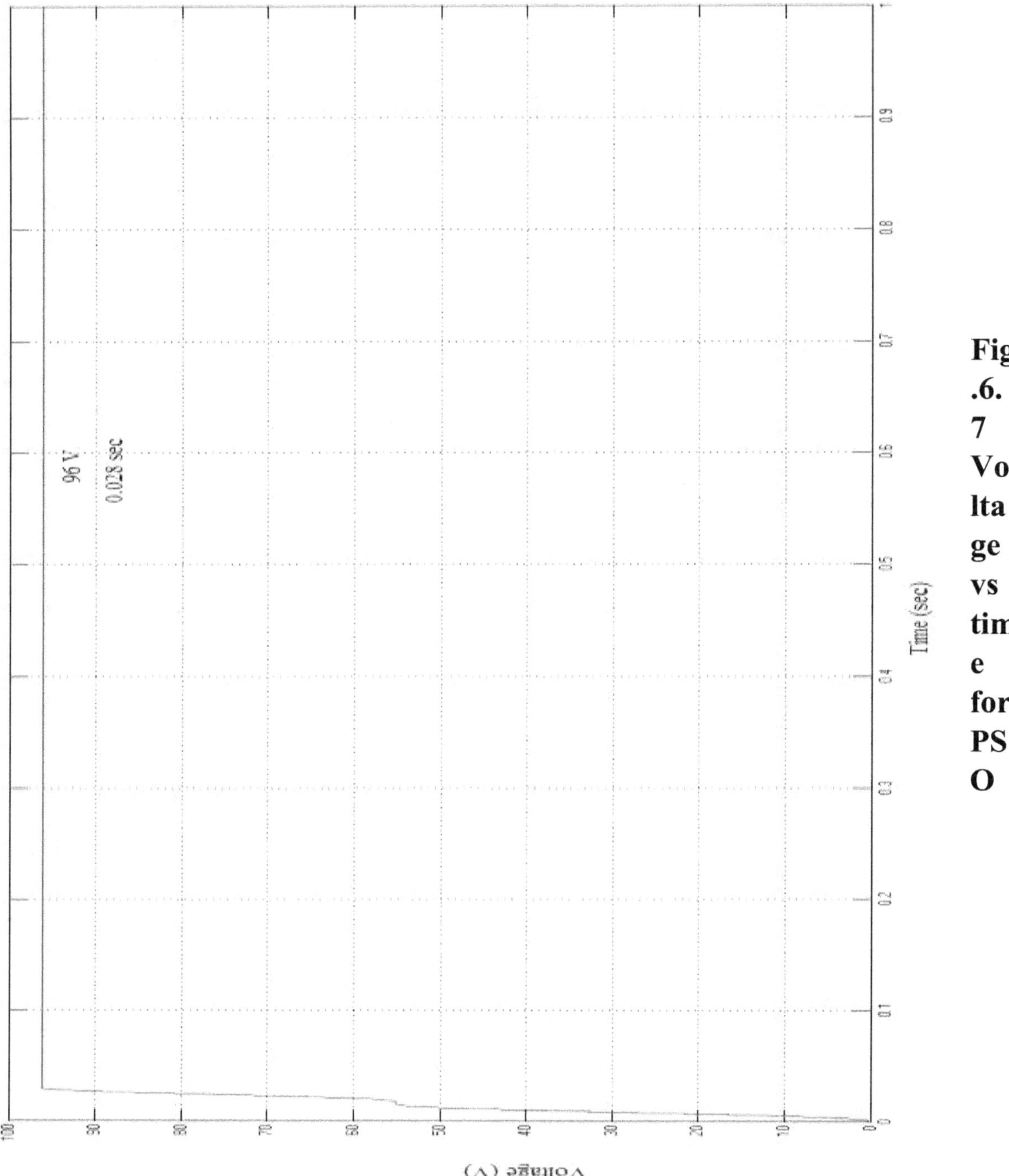

Fig.6.7 Voltage vs time for PSO

Output voltage= 96 V, Settling time= 0.028 sec

6.5 Simulation results for comparison of conventional P&O and PSO

Fig.6.8 shows the output waveforms for both conventional P&O and PSO. The inference is given below.

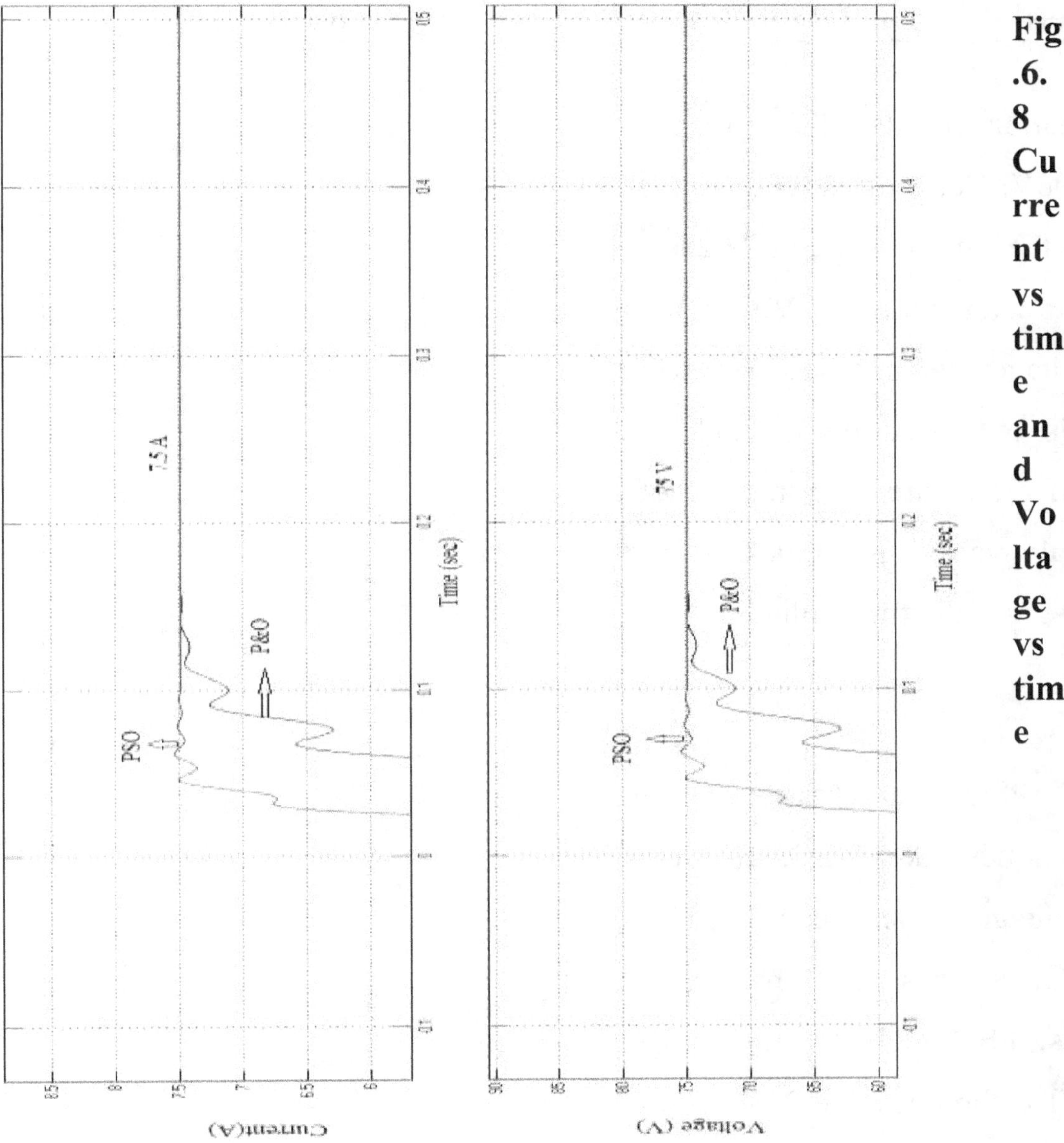

Fig.6.8 Current vs time and Voltage vs time

1. Output current= 7.5A ;Output voltage= 75V

2. Settling time- P&O= 0.15sec; PSO= 0.08 sec

Table 6.1: Simulation results forConventional P&O and PSO

Parameters	P&O	PSO
Voltage(V)	93	96
Time for final value(sec)	0.036	0.028
Comparison models	7.5A, 75V, 0.15 sec	7.5A, 75V, 0.08sec

From simulation results, PSO gives an output voltage of 96V. Conventional P&O gives 93V. PSO reaches the final voltage in 0.028sec, faster compared to conventional P&O which gives the final voltage in 0.035 sec. From the comparison models, output current of 7.5A and output voltage of 75V are obtained. P&O reaches the final value in 0.08sec and conventional P&O gives the final value in 0.15sec.

Therefore, PSO is faster than conventional techniques like P&O. It yields higher output voltage when compared to conventional P&O. It has also has faster convergence. Thus, PSO is better than other conventional MPPT techniques like P&O.

CHAPTER 7
HARDWARE IMPLEMENTATION OF MPPT BASED PV SYSTEM

Hardware implementation of MPPT based PV system has been done in this project. The block diagram, components used, miniaturized model and results are presented below.

7.1 Block diagram

The block diagram and schematic of the hardware model are shown below.

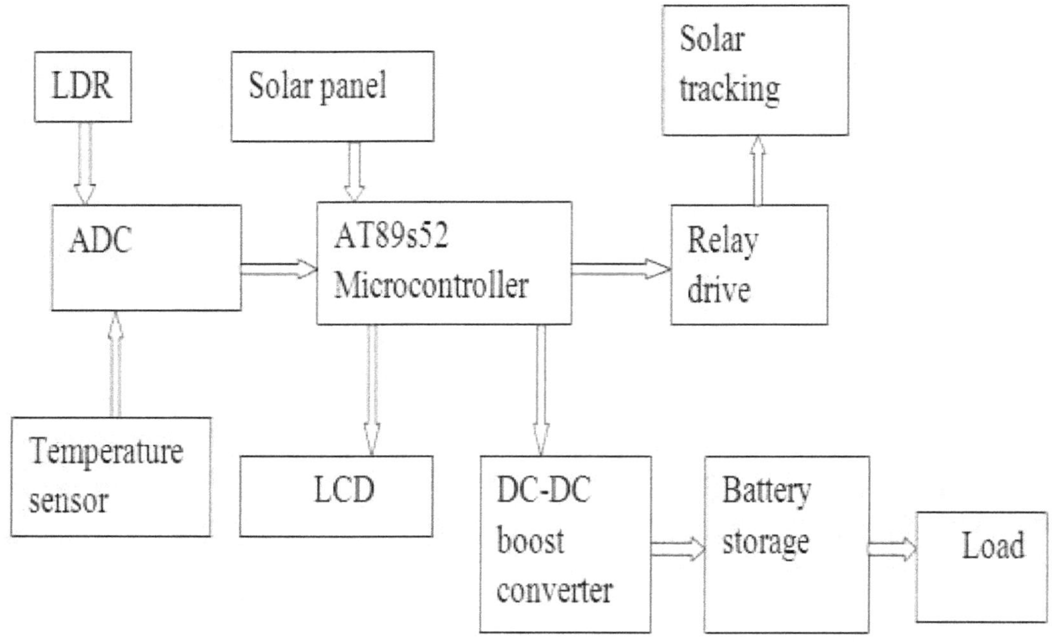

Fig.7.1 Block diagram

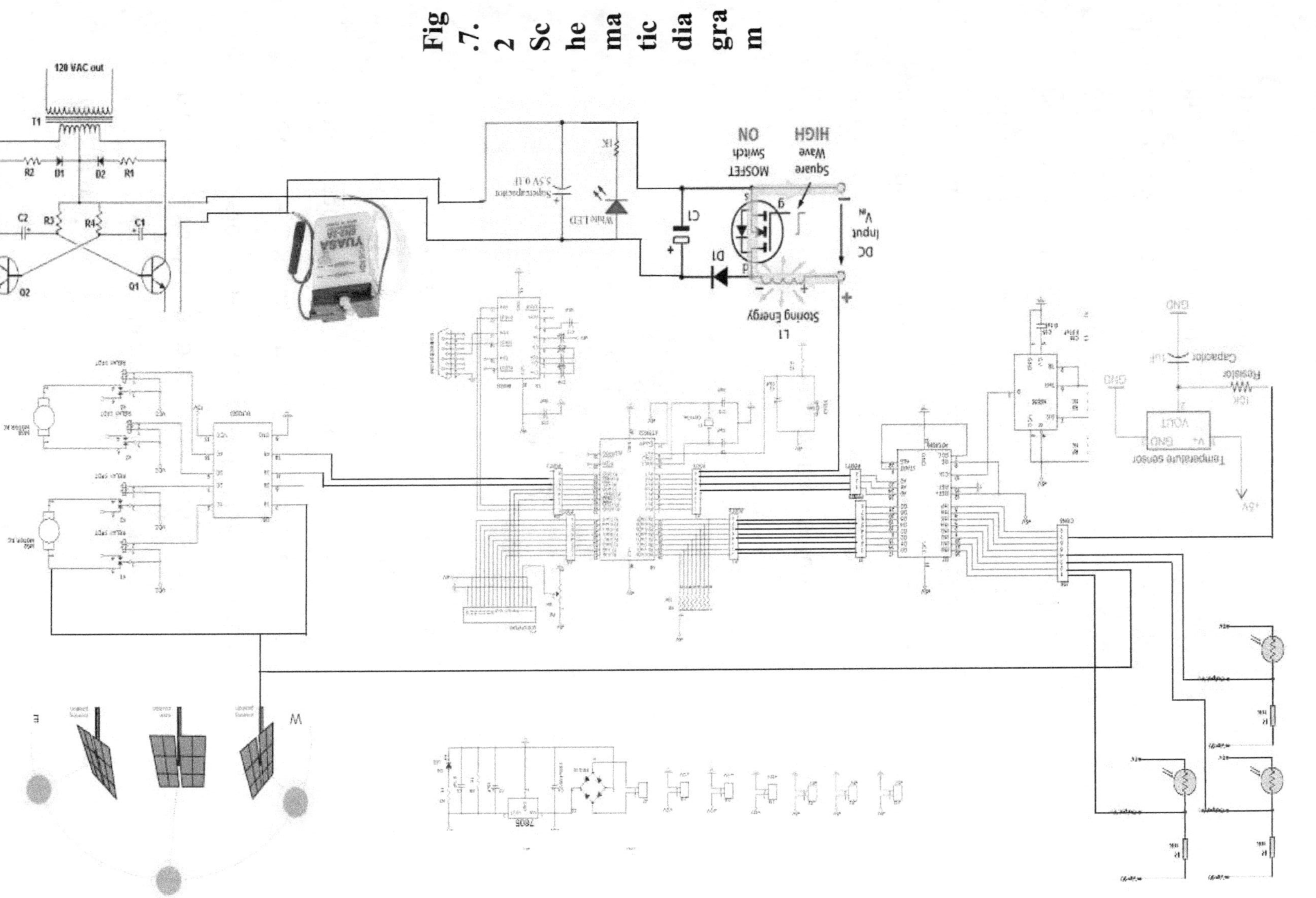

Fig .7.2 Schematic diagram

7.2 Solar Panel

A photovoltaic module or photovoltaic panel is a packaged interconnected assembly of photovoltaic cells. The photovoltaic module, known more commonly as the solar panel, is then used as a component in a larger photovoltaic system to offer electricity for commercial and residential applications

Fig.7.3. Solar Panel

Because a single photovoltaic module can only produce a certain amount of wattage, installations intended to produce larger electrical power capacity require an installation of several modules or panels and this is known as a photovoltaic array.Solar Panels use light energy (photons) from the sun to generate electricity through photovoltaic effect (this is the photo-electric effect). For the project, PV module has been considered.

Table 7.1: Specifications of PV module

Maximum Power	3W
V_{MPP}	8V
I_{MPP}	0.37A
V_{OC}	10.1V
I_{SC}	0.43A

7.3

AT8

9s52 Microcontroller

AT89s52 Microcontroller is used in this project. The AT89S52 is a lowpower, high-performance CMOS 8-bit microcontroller with 8K bytes of in-system programmable Flash memory. The device is manufactured using Atmel's highdensity nonvolatile memory technology and is compatible with the Industry standard 80C51 instruction set and pin out.

Fig.7.4 AT89s52 Microcontroller

Fig 7.4 shows the pin diagram of AT89s52. It is a 40 pin IC.4.0V to 5.5V is the operating range. Frequency ranges from 0 Hz to 33 MHz.It has 4 ports (Port 0, Port 1, Port2, Port 3).Port 0 is an 8-bit bidirectional I/O port.Port 1 is an 8-bit bidirectional I/O port with internal pull-ups. Similarly Port 2 and Port 3 are also 8bit bidirectional I/O ports with internal pull-ups.

7.3.1Pin configuration

The pin configuration is shown below.

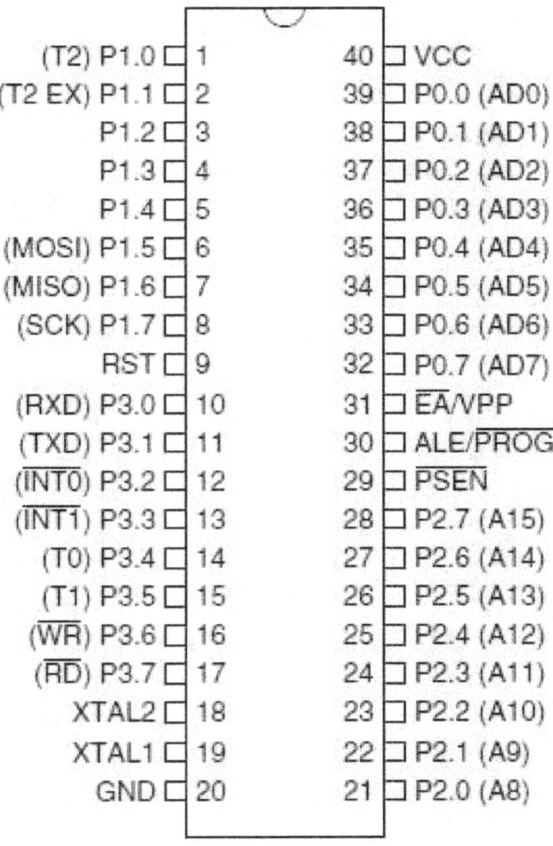

**Fig.7.5 Pin configuration of
AT89s52**

It receives information about the temperature, direction of light from ADC0809, and voltage generated by solar panel. Port 0 is used to receive this information. Port 2 is connected to the data lines of LCD. Pins P3.2, P3.3, P3.4 of Port 3 are connected to the control lines of LCD. Port 1 gives generated PWM signals to DC-DC boost converter. Pin details are given in Appendix 1.

Table 7.2: Functions of Port 3 pins

Port Pin	Alternate Functions
P3.0	RXD (serial input port)
P3.1	TXD (serial output port)
P3.2	INT0 (external interrupt 0)
P3.3	INT1 (external interrupt 1)
P3.4	T0 (timer 0 external input)
P3.5	T1 (timer 1 external input)
P3.6	WR (external data memory write strobe)
P3.7	RD (external data memory read strobe)

7.4 ADC 0809

ADC0809 data acquisition component is a monolithic CMOS device with an 8-bit analog-to-digital converter, 8-channel multiplexer and microprocessor compatible control logic. The 8-bit A/D converter uses successive approximation as the conversion technique.

Fig.7.6 ADC0809

The converter features a high impedance chopper stabilized comparator, a 256R voltage divider with analog switch tree and a successive approximation register.

The 8-channel multiplexer can directly access any of 8-single-ended analog signals.

7.4.1 Features

The feature are as follows

- Easy interface to all microprocessors.
- Operates ratio metrically or with 5 VDC or analog span
- 8-channel multiplexer with address logic
- 0V to 5V input range with single 5V power supply

7.4.2 Pin configuration

Fig 7.7 shows the pin configuration of ADC0809.

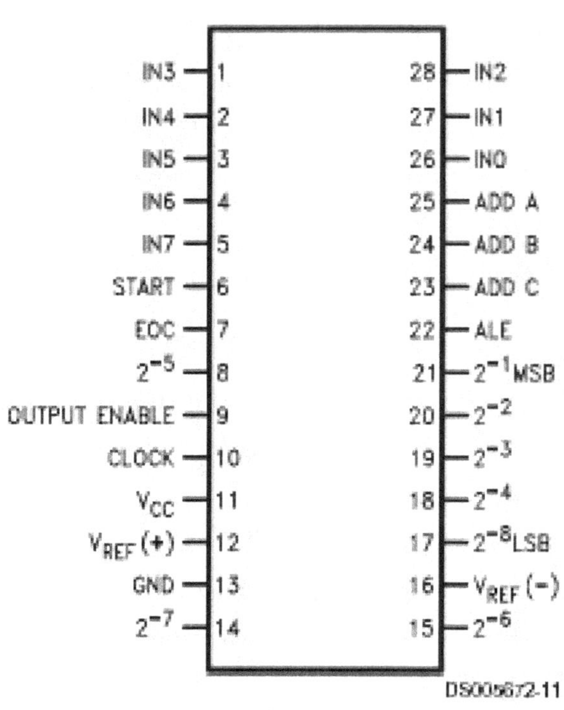

Fig 7.7 ADC0809 Pin configuration

ADC0809 receives input from LDR and Temperature sensor regarding the direction of light and temperature. It receives temperature input at channel 0. It converts analog data to digital and gives the same to microcontroller. 3 more channels are used to obtain information from 3 LDRs.

7.5 Temperature sensor

LM35 is a precision IC temperature sensor with its output proportional to the temperature (in ºC). The sensor circuitry is sealed and therefore it is not subjected to oxidation and other processes. With LM35, temperature can be measured more accurately than with a thermistor. It also possess low self heating and does not cause more than 0.1 ºC temperature rise in still air.

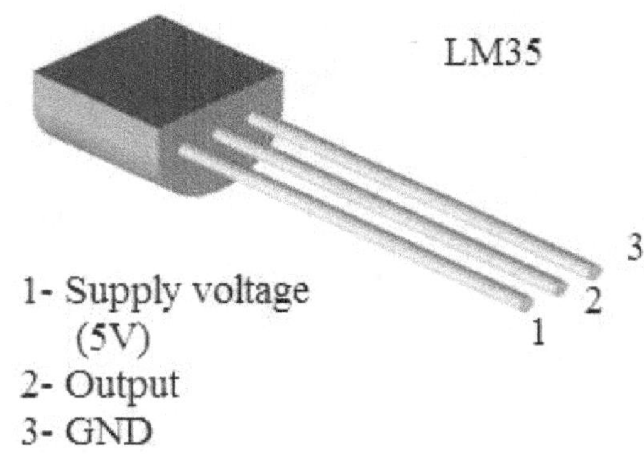

- Fig7.8 LM35.

The operating temperature range is from -55°C to 150°C. The output voltage varies by 10mV in response to every ºC rise/fall in ambient temperature,i.e., its scale factor is 0.01V/ ºC.The LM35's low output impedance, linear output, and precise inherent calibration make interfacing to readout or control circuitry especially easy.

It is used to detect temperature of the surroundings. Temperature is displayed on the LCD. Temperature is an analog input. It is converted to digital form by ADC.
It is connected channel 0 of ADC.

7

.

5.1 Features

The features ar

e

- Low cost due to wafer-level trimming.
- Operates from 4 to 30 volts.
- Less than 60 µA current drain.
- Low self-heating, 0.08°C in still air.
- Nonlinearity only ±¼°C typical.

7.5.2 Pin description

Pin1 is used for supply ranging from +35V to -2V. Usual supply voltage is 5V. Pin2 is used as output pin. Pin3 is used for ground.

7.6 LDR – Light Dependent Resistor

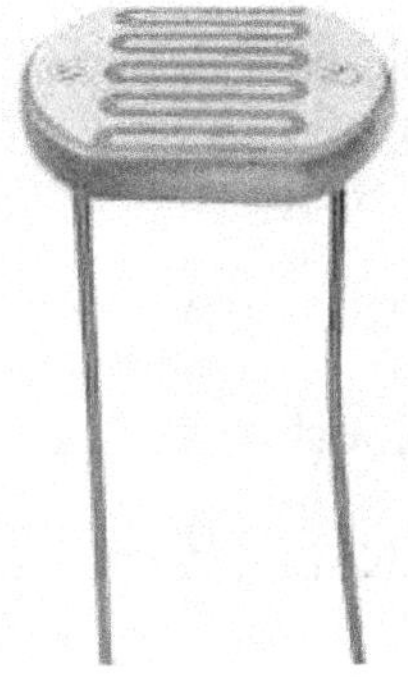

Fig 7.9 LDR

Light Dependent Resistors are very useful sensor especially in light/dark circuits. Normally the resistance of an LDR is very high, sometimes as high as 1000 000 ohms, but when they are illuminated with light resistance drops dramatically.It is made of a high resistance semiconductor. If light falling on the device is of high enough frequency, photons absorbed by the semiconductor give bound electrons enough energy to jump into the conduction band. The resulting free electron (and its hole partner) conduct electricity, thereby lowering resistance.

It has a transparent coating over the surface. It has two electrodes. Over the ceramic covering the CdS track acts like a pathway to detect light. There are two photoresistor terminals which are soldered to the ceramic covering. Fig.7.9 shows the parts of an LDR.

In this hardware, LDR is used to sense the direction of light. 3 LDRs are used in the hardware model, each for left, right and centre. The LDR detects the direction of light source. This analog input is given to ADC. This information is used to run a DC gear motor (12V, 100rpm) to position the panel to the direction of the sun.

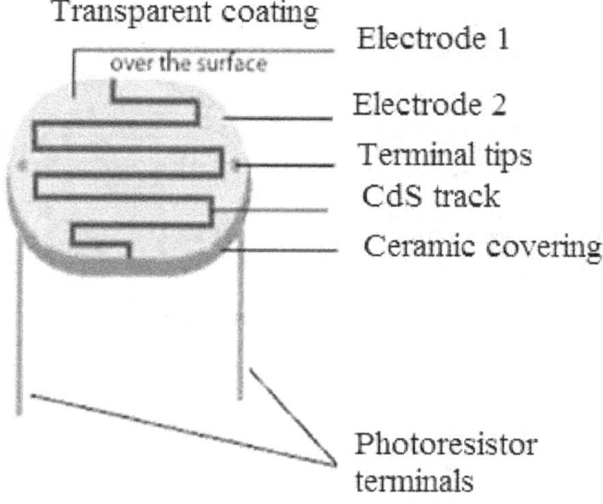

Fig 7.10 Parts of an LDR

7.7 Relay

A relay is an electrically operated switch. Current flowing through the coil of the relay creates a magnetic field which attracts a lever and changes the switch contacts.The coil current can be on or off so relays have two switch positions. There is no electrical connection inside the relay between the two circuits; the link is magnetic and mechanical.

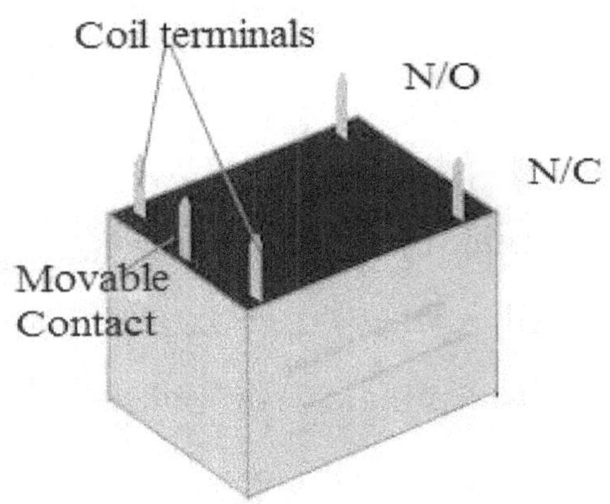

Fig 7.11 Relay

The coil of a relay passes a relatively large current, typically 30mA for a 12V relay, but it can be as much as 100mA for relays designed to operate from lower voltages. Most ICs (chips) cannot provide this current and a transistor is usually used to amplify the small IC current to the larger value required for the relay coil.

Table 7.3: Pin description of Relay

Pin	Function
1	NC
2	Coil terminal
3	Movable contact
4	Coil terminal
5	NO

Here, the relays receive information from microcontroller for changing states. Based on the information from LDRs, relays act to position the panel by driving the DC gear motor. Relays are driven using ULN2003, which is a relay driver, to enhance the signals from microcontroller.

7.7.1 Pin Description

Fig.7.11 shows the pins of a relay. Pin1 has No Connection (normally closed). Pin 2 and Pin 4 are connected to coil terminals. The pole is a movable contact and Pin 5 is Normally Open.

7.7.2 Features

- Selection of plastic material for high temperature and better chemical solution performance. Sealed types available.
- Simple relay magnetic circuit to meet low cost of mass production.
- Onboard relay counting.

- Operating Voltage: 12 Volts DC Nominal.

- Current Draw: 30 milliamps.

- Minimum Pull-in Voltage: 9 Volts DC.

7.8 ULN 2003 (Relay driver circuit)

The ULN2003 is a monolithic high voltage and high current Darlington transistor arrays. It consists of seven NPN Darlington pairs that features highvoltage outputs with common – cathodeclamp diode for switching inductive loads. The collector-current rating of a single Darlington pair is 500mA. ULN details are given in Appendix 2.

7.8.1 Pin configuration

The pin configuration of ULN2003 is given below.

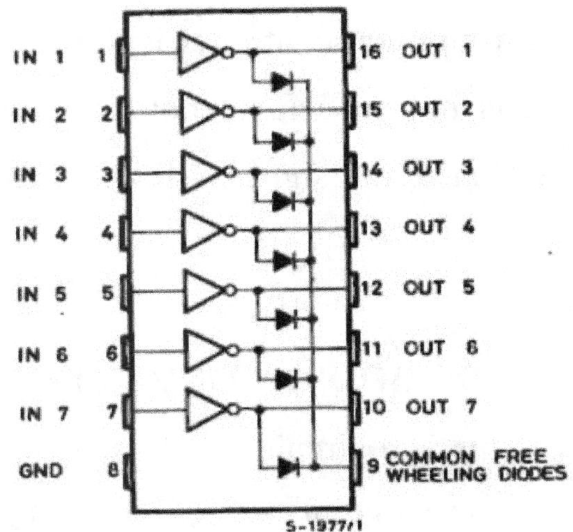

Fig 7.12 ULN2003 pin configuration

The Darlington pairs may be paralleled for higher current capability. Applications includerelay drivers,hamer drivers, lampdrivers,display drivers(LED gasdischarge),line drivers, and logic buffers.The ULN2003 has a 2.7kW series base resistor for eachDarlington pair for operation directlywith TTL or 5V CMOSdevices.

7.8.2 Features

- 500mA rated collector current (Single output)
- High-voltage outputs: 50V
- Inputs compatible with various types of logic.
- Relay driver application.

ULN2003 is used as a relay driver in the hardware model. This is because the output signal from microcontroller is low in magnitude and it is not sufficient enough to operate the relay. Hence, the signal is boosted to drive the relay.

7.9 DC- DC BOOST CONVERTER

This is a circuit which steps up the input voltage. The output voltage is greater than the input. The range of boosting used in this circuit is stepping up process from 5V to 12V DC. It is a circuit which has T0-220AB package

(MOSFET switch). MOSFET is used as a switching device. The output is stored in a super capacitor and is given to a battery. The battery is connected to an inverter unit and voltage is stepped up to give 180V AC. A lamp (load) can be connected to the output of the inverter. The circuit has been designed to boost 5V to 12 V. Microcontroller generates PWM signals which switch the MOSFET accordingly.

7.10 LCD Unit (Liquid Crystal Display)

The LCD model is LM016L. It has 3 control pins, 8 data pins,V_{SS},V_{DD}, LED+,LED-, V0. 5 V supply is given to LCD. It has a 16x2 display. Fig.10.13 shows an LCD model. Pin details are given in Appendix 3.

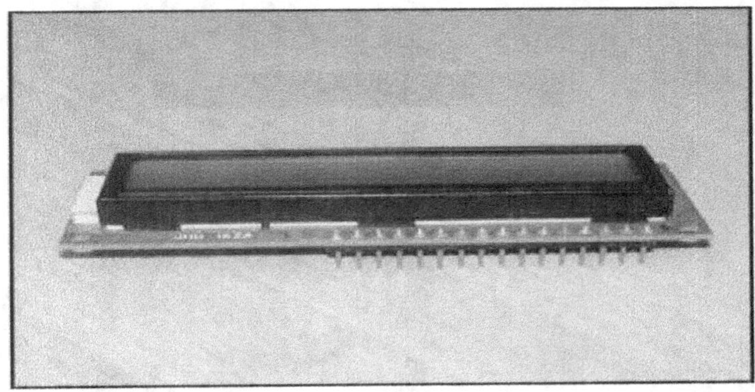

Fig.7.13 LCD

LCD is an output device which is used to display output values. LCD is connected to Port 2 of microcontroller. Hence Port 2 is used as an output port. It has two modes: Command mode and data mode. It displays values corresponding to 3 LDRs (left, right and centre denoted as L,R and C respectively), temperature (T from LM35) , Solar panel output (denoted by S) and battery voltage (B). When the amount of sunlight that falls on the panel varies, S output varies. Similarly, according to the direction of light, the values of L, R and C vary.

7.11 Miniaturized model of MPPT based PV system

Fig 7.14 shows the miniaturized model implemented for this project.

Fig.7.14 Miniaturized model

1. Solar panel
2. LDRs
3. Relay
4. LCD unit
5. Microcontroller
6. Panel positioning using DC motor
7. 12V Battery

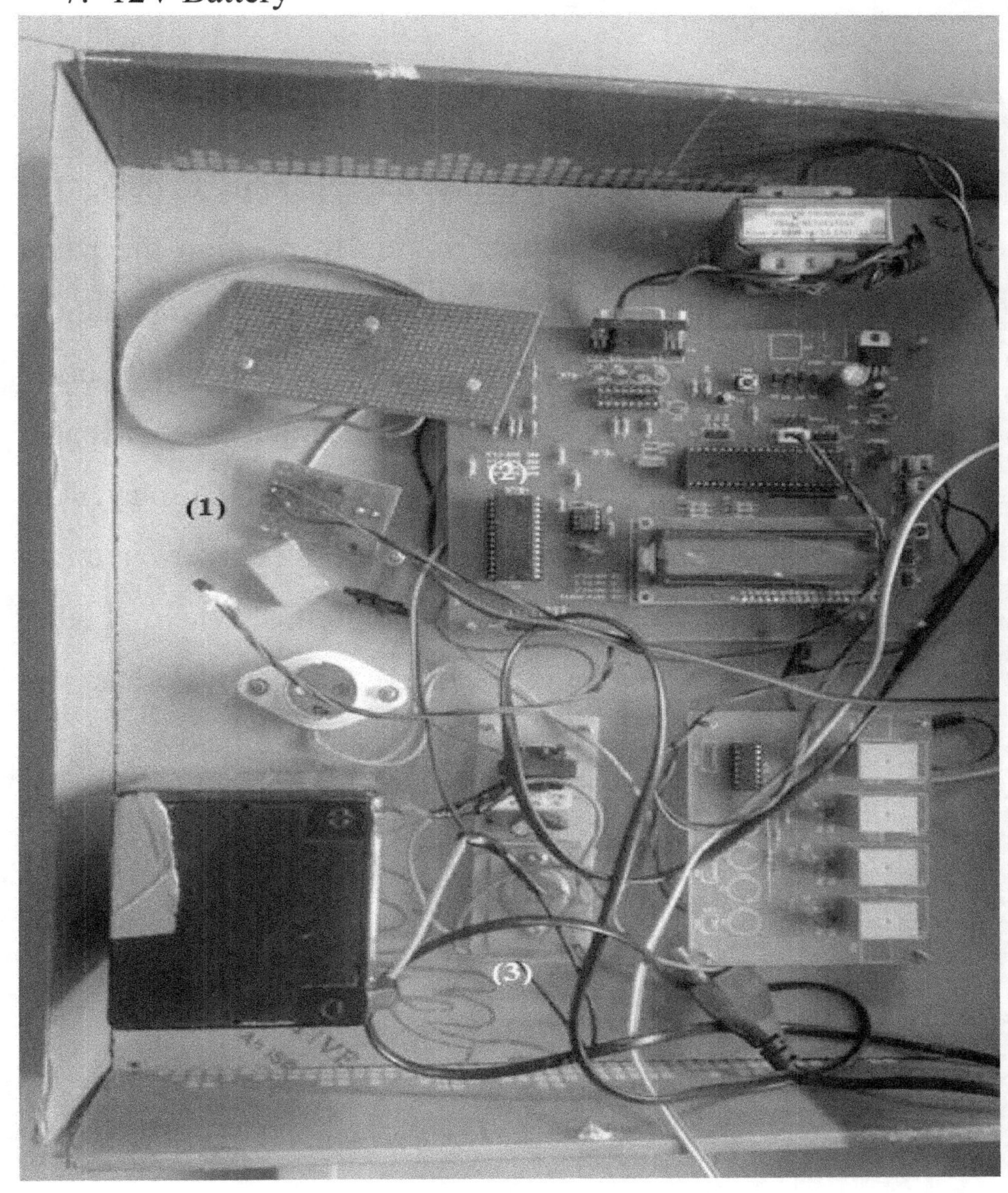

**Fig.7.15
Hardware
implementation**

1. DC-DC boost converter

2. ADC0809

3. Inverter unit

This modelhas the capability to detect the direction of light source to position the panel accordingly. Temperature of the surrounding is also detected. Partial shading condition can be detected according to the output of solar panel which can be seen on the LCD display. The output of boost converter is 12V even under partial shading conditions. When higher irradiation is received, the model has the capability to charge the battery directly.

CHAPTER 8

RESULTS, CONCLUSION
AND FUTURE WORK

The following table from Table 6.1 shows the simulation results.

Simulation results for MPPT based PV system

Parameters	P&O	PSO
Voltage(V)	93	96
Settling time (sec)	0.036	0.028
Comparison models	7.5A, 75V, 0.15 sec	7.5A, 75V, 0.08sec

PSO gives an output voltage of 96V. Conventional P&O gives 93V. PSO reaches the final voltage in 0.028sec, faster compared to conventional P&O which gives the final voltage in 0.035 sec. From the comparison models, output current of 7.5A and output voltage of 75V are obtained. P&O reaches the final value in

0.08sec and conventional P&O gives the final value in 0.15sec.

The miniaturized model has the capability to detect the direction of light source to position the panel accordingly. Temperature of the surrounding is also detected. Partial shading condition can detected. This is according to the output of solar panel. This model can display this detail on the LCD display. The output of boost converter is 12V even under partial shading conditions.

Conclusion

PSO is better than conventional techniques like P&O. PSO is faster and converges to the final value of output voltage in less time compared to conventional P&O. PSO yields higher output voltage when compared to conventional P&O. PSO works even under partial shading conditions. Hence PSO is the MPPT technique to be used under partial shading conditions for PV systems.

Future work

This project has shown that PSO is better than conventional techniques like P&O. Other conventional techniques are Incremental conductance, Fractional Open Circuit Voltage method, Fractional Short Circuit Current method, etc.

Future scope of this project can be improvising on the existing PSO algorithms. PSO can be implemented along with P&O or INC to create hybrid algorithms. These algorithms are becoming popular fields of research.

Improved PSO can be obtained by finding out ways to optimize the parameters of PSO like weight inertia, acceleration factors, random numbers etc. Dynamic assignment of constants is also a field of study. Reducing the complexity of existing methods is also suggested.

Real time implementation of these algorithms is the future work of this project.

REFERENCES

[1] Ahmed. F. Zobaa, Ramdan B. A. Koad, (2014), "Comparison between theConventional Methods and PSO Based MPPT Algorithm for PhotovoltaicSystems," World Academy of Science, Engineering and Technology, International Journal of Electrical, Computer, Electronics and Communication Engineering Vol: 8 No: 4.

[2] Ali Nasr Allah Ali, Mohamed H. Saied, M. Z. Mostafa, T. M. Abdel-Moneim, (2012), "A Survey of Maximum PPT techniques of PV Systems," Browse Conference Publications, Energytech, IEEE.

[3] Bidyadhar Subudhi and Raseswari Pradhan, (JANUARY 2013), "A Comparative Study on Maximum Power Point Tracking Techniques for Photovoltaic Power Systems," IEEE TRANSACTIONS ON SUSTAINABLE ENERGY, VOL. 4, NO. 1.

[4] David Sanz Morales (2010), "Maximum Power Point Tracking

Algorithms for Photovoltaic Applications" Thesis submitted for the examination of degree of Master of Science and Technology, Aalto University.

[5] DOLARA, R. FARANDA and S. LEVA, (2009), "Energy Comparison of Seven MPPT Techniques for PV Systems," Journal ofElectromagnetic Analysis and Applications, Vol.1, No.3, pp. 152-162.

[6] Eftichios Koutroulis, Kostas Kalaitzakis, Member, IEEE, and Nicholas C.
Voulgaris, (JANUARY 2001), "Development of a Microcontroller-Based
Photovoltaic Maximum Power Point TrackingControl System,International Journal of Electrical, Computer, Electronics and Communication Engineering Vol: 8 No:4.

[7] Imran Ali, Travis Comer, Keith Walls(2012)," Tohoku Relief Project – Wind/Solar Energy Power Generator", Workforce Central Florida, Progress Energy Symposium.

[8] Kinal Kachhiya, Makarand Lokhande, (May 2011), "MATLAB/Simulink Model of Solar PV Module and MPPT Algorithm", National Conference on Recent Trends in Engineering & Technology, 13-14 B.V.M. Engineering College, V.V.Nagar, Gujarat, India.

[9] Mida Dris, Benattous Djilani, (2013), "Comparative Study of Algorithms

(MPPT) Applied to Photovoltaic Systems", INTERNATIONAL JOURNAL of RENEWABLE ENERGY RESEARCH Benattous Djilani et al., Vol.3, No.4.

[10] Mohamed A. El-Sayed 1 and Steven Leeb2, (April 2014), "Evaluation of Maximum Power Point Tracking Algorithms for Photovoltaic Electricity Generation in Kuwait", International Conference on Renewable Energies and Power Quality (ICREPQ'14) Cordoba (Spain), 8th to 10th April, 2014, Renewable Energy and Power Quality Journal (RE&PQJ), ISSN 2172-038 X, No.12.

[11] Mohammad Sarvi, Mandana Hojati Tabatabaee, Iman Soltani, (2014), "A Fast Maximum Power Point Tracking for mismatching compensation for PV Systems under Normal and Partially Shaded Conditions", Journal of mathematics and computer science 8, 52-74

[12] Mohammad Sarvi, Saeedeh Ahmadi and Shirzad Abdi (2013), "A PSObased maximum power point tracking for photovoltaic systems under environmental and partially shaded conditions", PROGRESS IN PHOTOVOLTAICS: RESEARCH AND APPLICATIONS, Prog. Photovolt: Res. Appl. Published online in Wiley Online Library (wileyonlinelibrary.com). DOI: 10.1002/pip.2416

[13] Mohammadmehdi Seyedmahmoudian, Saad Mekhilef, Rasoul Rahmani, Rubiyah Yusof, and Ali Asghar Shojaei, (2014), "Maximum power point tracking of partial shaded photovoltaic array using an evolutionary algorithm: A particle swarm optimization technique" Journal of Renewable and Sustainable Energy 6, 023102 AIP PublishingPhotovoltaic Maximum Power Point Tracking Control System", IEEE TRANSACTIONS ON POWER ELECTRONICS, VOL. 16, NO. 1.

[14] Qinghai Bai, (Feb 2010), Analysis of Particle Swarm Optimization Algorithm, Computer and information science, Vol3, No.1.

[15] R. El. Gouri,M.Ben Brahim, H. Hlou, (20th December 2013), " A comparative study of MPPT technical based on fuzzy logic and perturb observe algorithms for photovoltaic systems," Journal of theoretical and Applied Information Technology, Vol 58 .No.2.

[16] Rahul Suryavanshi, Diwakar R. Joshi, Suresh H. Jangamshetti, (March 2012), "PSO and P&O based MPPT Technique for SPV Panel under Varying Atmospheric Conditions," International Journal of Engineering and Innovative Technology (IJEIT) Volume 1, Issue 3.

[17] Ramdan B. A. Koad, Ahmed. F. Zobaa, (2014), "Comparison between the Conventional Methods and PSO Based MPPT Algorithm for Photovoltaic Systems", World Academy of Science, Engineering and Technology

[18] S.Gomathy, S.Saravanan, Dr. S. Thangavel, (March -2012), "Design and Implementation of Maximum Power Point Tracking (MPPT) Algorithm for a Standalone PV System", International Journal of Scientific & Engineering Research Volume 3, Issue 3, 1 ISSN 2229-5518 IJSER.

[19] Selvapriyanka. P, Vijayakumar. G, (January 2014), "Particle Swarm Optimization Based MPPT for PV System under Partial Shading Conditions", International Journal of Innovative Research in Science, Engineering and Technology, An ISO 3297: 2007 Certified Organization, Volume 3, Special Issue 1, International Conference on Engineering Technology and Science-(ICETS'14)

[20] T. Esram, P. L. Chapman, (June 2007), "Comparison of Photovoltaic Array Maximum Power Point Tracking Techniques," IEEE Transactions on Energy Conversion, vol. 22, no. 2, pp. 439-449.

[21] V. Salas, E. Olías, A. Barrado, and A. Lázaro, (2006), "Review of the maximum power point tracking algorithms for stand-alone photovoltaic systems", ELSEVIER,Science Direct, Solar Energy Materials & Solar Cells vol.90, 1555–1578.

APPENDIX 1

AT89S52 Microcontroller

Features:

- Compatible with MCS-51® Products
- 8K Bytes of In-System Programmable (ISP) Flash Memory
- 4.0V to 5.5V Operating Range
- Fully Static Operation: 0 Hz to 33 MHz
- Three-level Program Memory Lock
- 256 x 8-bit Internal RAM
- 32 Programmable I/O Lines
- Three 16-bit Timer/Counters
- Eight Interrupt Sources
- Full Duplex UART Serial Channel
- Low-power Idle and Power-down Modes
- Interrupt Recovery from Power-down Mode
- Watchdog Timer
- Dual Data Pointer
- Power-off Flag

Description:

The AT89S52 is a low-power, high-performance CMOS 8-bit microcontroller with 8K bytes of in-system programmable Flash memory. The device is manufactured using Atmel's high-density nonvolatile memory technology and is compatible with the industry-standard 80C51 instruction set and pin out. The on-chip Flash allows the program memory to be reprogrammed in-system or by a conventional nonvolatile memory programmer. By combining a versatile 8-bit CPU with insystem programmable Flash on a monolithic chip, the Atmel AT89S52 is a powerful microcontroller which provides a highly-flexible and cost-effective solution to many embedded control applications

P
i
n

D
e
s
c
r
i
p
t
i
o
n

Vcc Supply voltage.

GND Ground.

Port 0

Port 0 is an 8-bit open drain bidirectional I/O port. As an output port, each pin can sink eight TTL inputs. When 1s are written to port 0 pins, the pins can be used as high impedance inputs. Port 0 can also be configured to be the multiplexed low order address/data bus during accesses to external program and data memory. In this mode, P0 has internal pull-ups. Port 0 also receives the code bytes during Flash programming and outputs the code bytes during program verification. External pull-ups are required during program verification.

Port 1

Port 1 is an 8-bit bidirectional I/O port with internal pull-ups. The Port 1 output buffers can sink/source four TTL inputs. When 1s are written to Port 1 pins, they are pulled high by the internal pull-ups and can be used as inputs. As inputs, Port 1 pins that are externally being pulled low will source current (IIL) because of the internal pull-ups. In addition, P1.0 and P1.1 can be configured to be the timer/counter 2 external count input (P1.0/T2) and the timer/counter 2 trigger input (P1.1/T2EX), respectively, as shown in the following table. Port 1 also receives the low-order address bytes during Flash programming and verification.

PORT 1　　　　　　　**Function of Port 1 pins**

Port Pin	Alternate Functions

P1.0	T2 (external count input to Timer/Counter 2), clock-out
P1.1	T2EX (Timer/Counter 2 capture/reload trigger and direction control)
P1.5	MOSI (used for In-System Programming)
P1.6	MISO (used for In-System Programming)
P1.7	SCK (used for In-System Programming)

Port 2

Port 2 is an 8-bit bidirectional I/O port with internal pull-ups. The Port 2 output buffers can sink/source four TTL inputs. When 1s are written to Port 2 pins, they are pulled high by the internal pull-ups and can be used as inputs. As inputs, Port 2 pins that are externally being pulled low will source current (I_{IL}) because of the internal pull-ups. Port 2 emits the high-order address byte during fetches from external program memory and during accesses to external data memory that use 16bit addresses (MOVX @ DPTR). In this application, Port 2 uses strong internal pull-ups when emitting 1s. During accesses to external data memory that use 8-bit addresses (MOVX @ RI), Port 2 emits the contents of the P2 Special Function Register. Port 2 also receives the high-order address bits and some control signals during Flash programming and verification.

Port 3

Port 3 is an 8-bit bidirectional I/O port with internal pull-ups. The Port 3 output buffers can sink/source four TTL inputs. When 1s are written to Port 3 pins, they are pulled high by the internal pull-ups and can be used as inputs. As inputs, Port 3 pins that are externally being pulled low will source current (I_{IL}) because of the pull-ups. Port 3 also serves the functions of various special features of the AT89S52, as shown in the following table. Port 3 also receives some control signals for Flash programming and verification.

PORT 3 pins **Function of Port 3**

Port Pin	Alternate Functions
P3.0	RXD (serial input port)
P3.1	TXD (serial output port)
P3.2	INT0 (external interrupt 0)
P3.3	INT1 (external interrupt 1)
P3.4	T0 (timer 0 external input)

P3.5	T1 (timer 1 external input)
P3.6	WR (external data memory write strobe)
P3.7	RD (external data memory read strobe)

RST

Reset input. A high on this pin for two machine cycles while the oscillator is running resets the device. This pin drives High for 96 oscillator periods after the Watchdog times out. The DISRTO bit in SFR AUXR (address 8EH) can be used to disable this feature. In the default state of bit DISRTO, the RESET HIGH out feature is enabled.

ALE/PROG ⎯⎯

Address Latch Enable (ALE) is an output pulse for latching the low byte of the address during accesses to external memory. This pin is also the program pulse input (PROG) during Flash programming . In normal operation, ALE is emitted at a constant rate of 1/6 the oscillator frequency and may be used for external timing or clocking purposes. Note, however, that one ALE pulse is skipped during each access to external data memory. If desired, ALE operation can be disabled by setting bit 0 of

SFR location 8EH. With the bit set, ALE is active only during a

MOVX or MOVC instruction. Otherwise, the pin is weakly pulled high. Setting the ALE-disable bit has no effect if the microcontroller is in external execution mode.

PSEN

Program Store Enable (PSEN) is the read strobe to external program memory. When the AT89S52 is executing code from external program memory, PSEN is activated twice each machine cycle, except that two PSEN activations are skipped during each access to external data memory.

EA/VPP

External Access Enable. EA must be strapped to GND in order to enable the device to fetch code from external program memory locations starting at 0000H up to FFFFH. Note, however, that if lock bit 1 is programmed, EA will be internally latched on reset. EA should be strapped to VCC for internal program executions. This pin also receives the 12-volt programming enable voltage (VPP) during Flash programming.

XTAL1

Input to the inverting oscillator amplifier and input to the internal clock operating circuit.

XTAL2

Output from the inverting oscillator amplifier

APPENDIX 2 ULN2003 Features

- Seven Darlingtons per package

- Output current 500 mA per driver (600 mA peak)

- Output voltage 50 V

- Integrated suppression diodes for inductive loads

- Outputs can be paralleled for higher current

- TTL/CMOS/PMOS/DTL compatible inputs

- Inputs pinned opposite outputs to simplify layout

Description

The ULN2003 is a high voltage , high current Darlington array each containing seven open collector Darlington pairs with common emitters. Each channel rated at 500 mA and can withstand peak currents of 600 mA.
Suppression diodes are included for inductive load driving and the inputs are pinned opposite the outputs to simplify board layout.

These versatile devices are useful for driving a wide range of loads including solenoids, relays DC motors, LED displays filament lamps, thermal printheads and high power buffers.

Schematic diagram

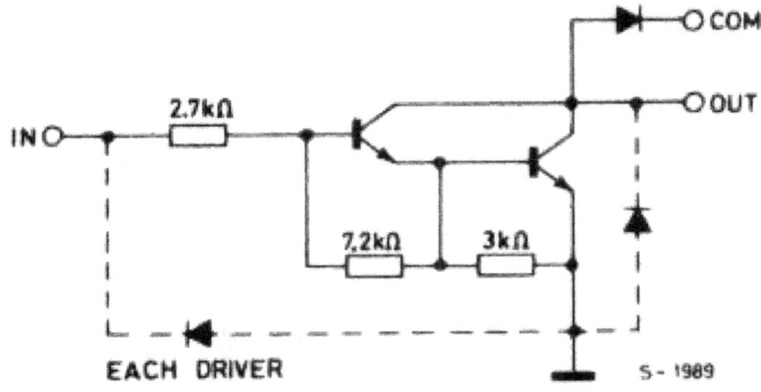

Maximum ratings:

Absolute maximum ratings

Symbol	Parameter	Value	Unit
V_O	Output voltage	50	V
V_I	Input voltage (for ULN2002A/D - 2003A/D - 2004A/D)	30	V
I_C	Continuous collector current	500	mA
I_B	Continuous base current	25	mA
T_A	Operating ambient temperature range	- 40 to 85	°C
T_{STG}	Storage temperature range	- 55 to 150	°C
T_J	Junction temperature	150	°C

Thermal data

Symbol	Parameter	DIP-16	SO-16	Unit
R_{thja}	Thermal resistance junctionambient, Max.	70	120	□C/W

Electrical Characteristics

Symbol	Parameter	Test condition	Min.	Typ.	Max.	Unit
I_{CEX}	Output leakage current	$V_{CE} = 50$ V,			50	μA
		$T_A = 85°C$, $V_{CE} = 50$ V			100	
		$T_A = 85°C$ for ULN2002, $V_{CE} = 50$ V, $V_I = 6$ V			500	
		$T_A = 85°C$ for ULN2002, $V_{CE} = 50$ V, $V_I = 1$V			500	
V_{CE}	Collector-emitter saturation Voltage	$I_C = 100$ mA, $I_B = 250$ μA		0.9	1.1	V
		$I_C = 200$ mA, $I_B = 350$ μA		1.1	1.3	
		$I_C = 350$ mA, $I_B = 500$ μA		1.3	1.6	
$I_I(ON)$	Input current	for ULN2002, $V_I = 17$ V		0.82	1.25	mA
		for ULN2003, $V_I = 3.85$ V		0.93	1.35	
		for ULN2004, $V_I = 5$ V		0.35	0.5	
		$V_I = 12$ V		1	1.45	
$I_I(OFF)$	Input current	$T_A = 85°C$, $I_C = 500$ μA	50	65		μA
$V_I(ON)$	Input voltage	$V_{CE} = 2$ V, for ULN2002 $I_C = 300$ mA			13	V
		for ULN2003 $I_C = 200$ mA			2.4	
		$I_C = 250$ mA			2.7	
		$I_C = 300$ mA			3	
		for ULN2004 $I_C = 125$ mA			5	
		$I_C = 200$ mA			6	
		$I_C = 275$ mA			7	
		$I_C = 350$ mA			8	
h_{FE}	DC Forward current gain	for ULN2001, $V_{CE} = 2$ V, $I_C = 350$ mA	1000			
C_I	Input capacitance			15	25	pF
t_{PLH}	Turn-on delay time	$0.5 V_I$ to $0.5 V_O$		0.25	1	μs
t_{PHL}	Turn-off delay time	$0.5 V_I$ to $0.5 V_O$		0.25	1	μs
I_R	Clamp diode leakage current	$V_R = 50$ V			50	μA
		$T_A = 85°C$, $V_R = 50$ V			100	

V_F	Clamp diode forward voltage	$I_F = 350$ mA			1.7	2	V

PIN NO.	NAME	FUNCTION
1	VSS	Ground voltage
2	VCC	+5V
3	VEE	Contrast voltage
4	RS	Register select 0=Instruction Register 1=Data Register
5	R/W	Read/Write, to choose read or write mode 0=write mode 1=read mode
6	E	Enable 0=start to latch data to LCD character 1=disable
7	DB0	Data bit 0 (LSB)
8	DB1	Data bit 1
9	DB2	Data bit 2
10	DB3	Data bit 3
11	DB4	Data bit 4
12	DB5	Data bit 5
13	DB6	Data bit 6
14	DB7	Data bit 7 (MSB)
15	BPL	Back Pane Light +5V or lower (optional)
16	GND	Ground voltage (optional)

<table>
<tr><td></td><td></td><td></td></tr>
</table>

APPENDIX 3 LCD PIN details
Electrical characteristics

Ta	....	25 (ºC)
V_{DD}	....	5.0 ± 0.25 V
Input high voltage	....	2.2V min
Input low voltage	....	0.6V max
Output high voltage	....	2.4V min
Output low voltage	....	0.4V max
Power supply current	....	1.0 (3.0mA-max)

Absolute maximum ratings

	Min	Max
Power supply for logic	0	6.5V
Power supply for LCD drive	0	6.5V
Operating temperature(ºC)	0	40
Storage temperature(ºC)	-20	60

Power Supply for LCD drive

Range for Vdd-Vo	....	1.5V to 5.25V
Ta=0 ºC	....	4.6 V
Ta=25 ºC	....	4.4 V
Ta=50 ºC	....	4.2 V